Essex County Greenbelt
Conserving our open space heritage

The Greenbelt Guidebook

A Guide to the Best Hikes,
River Trips and Natural History
of the
Essex County Greenbelt Association

*"When one tugs at a single thing in nature,
he finds it attached to the rest of the world."*
—John Muir

Supported by funding from:
The Horizon Foundation
Susanna Colloredo

The Greenbelt Guidebook
A Guide to the Best Hikes, River Trips and Natural History
of the Essex County Greenbelt Association

Fourth Edition ©2002 Essex County Greenbelt Association, Inc.
All rights reserved.

ISBN# 0-9719668-0-X
Price: $15.00 U.S.

Photographs by Dorothy Kerper Monnelly   ©2002 Essex County Greenbelt Association, Inc.
Photographs by Jim MacDougall   ©2002 Essex County Greenbelt Association, Inc.
Maps by Richard H. Sanderson   ©2002 Essex County Greenbelt Association, Inc.
Illustrations by Sandra Hogan McDermott   ©2000 Sandra Hogan McDermott
Illustrations by Cindy Mom   ©2002 Essex County Greenbelt Association, Inc.

Published by: Essex County Greenbelt Association, Inc.
                  82 Eastern Avenue, Essex, MA 01929

                  Telephone: 978-768-7241
                  Fax: 978-768-3286
                  E-Mail: ecga@ecga.org
                  Website: www.ecga.org

Property Maps: Richard H. Sanderson
Graphic Design: Keith Phelan, Phelan Design Studio
Printing: The Pressroom, Inc.

ACKNOWLEDGMENTS

The Fourth Edition of *The Greenbelt Guidebook* is the work of many volunteers, staff, and other contributors. The listing below represents those individuals who worked most actively on this edition.

Contributing Writers:	Jim MacDougall
	Cindy Mom
Editors:	Jim Berry Lisa Press
	Jill Buchanan David Rimmer
	Cindy Mom Julie Towne
Photography:	Dorothy Kerper Monnelly
	Jim MacDougall
Illustrations:	Sandra Hogan McDermott
	Cindy Mom

Greenbelt would like to specially thank the artists whose generous contributions of time and talent are featured throughout *The Guidebook*: Dorothy Kerper Monnelly for her landscape photographs, and Sandra Hogan McDermott and Cindy Mom for their illustrations of plants, animals, and birds. Greenbelt gratefully acknowledges the generosity of The Horizon Foundation and of Susanna Colloredo for funding support for *The Greenbelt Guidebook*.

We would like to particularly recognize Jim MacDougall, who conceived of and single-handedly wrote the complete text of the original *Passport to Essex County Greenbelt: A Guide to Open Space in Essex County* in 1983. Jim served as Land Manager from 1981 until October 2000, and it is his passionate love of the natural world and intimate knowledge of the properties gained through years of land stewardship which serve as the foundation of this *Guidebook*.

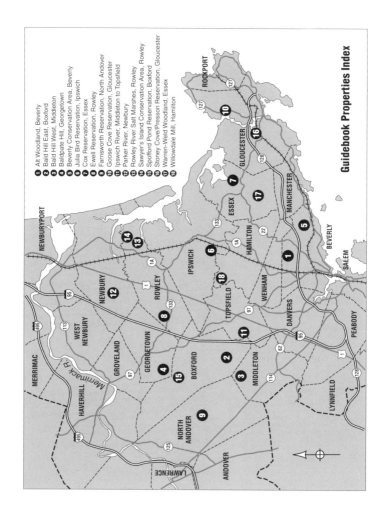

Guidebook Properties Index

1. Ait Woodland, Beverly
2. Bald Hill East, Boxford
3. Bald Hill West, Middleton
4. Baldpate Hill, Georgetown
5. Beverly Conservation Area, Beverly
6. Julia Bird Reservation, Ipswich
7. Cox Reservation, Essex
8. Ewell Reservation, Rowley
9. Farnsworth Reservation, North Andover
10. Goose Cove Reservation, Gloucester
11. Ipswich River, Middleton to Topsfield
12. Parker River, Newbury
13. Rowley River Salt Marshes, Rowley
14. Sawyer's Island Conservation Area, Rowley
15. Spofford Pond Reservation, Boxford
16. Stoney Cove/Presson Reservation, Gloucester
17. Warren-Weld Woodland, Essex
18. Willowdale Mill, Hamilton

4

CONTENTS

FEATURED GREENBELT PROPERTIES

APPENDIX

INTRODUCTION

Welcome to a world of beautiful rolling hills, whispering marsh grasses, serene woods, and rocky shores! *The Greenbelt Guidebook* offers you entrance into some of the best hikes, river trips and natural history of Essex County Greenbelt Association properties. These special natural areas have been protected forever as open space through the land conservation work of Greenbelt, and are available for you to enjoy, whether you wish to hike, fish, observe nature, mountain bike, ride horseback, cross-country ski, snowshoe, canoe, kayak, or picnic.

For over four decades, Greenbelt, a nonprofit land trust, has been conserving land of ecological, agricultural and scenic significance throughout Essex County, and last year we surpassed the milestone of 10,000 acres of land protected. By conserving the open space heritage of Essex County, we help ensure that future generations will continue to enjoy this key aspect of our quality of life.

We hope you will use *The Greenbelt Guidebook* to become better acquainted with the beauty and diversity which surrounds us every day. We also hope that you will be encouraged and inspired to see what has been achieved over the last forty years, and what is possible when members of the community work together with vision and dedication.

Ed Becker

Edward O. Becker
Executive Director
Essex, Massachusetts
January, 2002

ABOUT GREENBELT

In 1961, several farsighted citizens banded together with a vision to protect a beautiful 240-acre farm in Boxford known as Bald Hill. Out of that action evolved the Essex County Greenbelt Association, one of the most successful land trusts in the country.

As a private, nonprofit land trust, Greenbelt works to acquire open space in Essex County that has ecological, agricultural, or scenic significance, placing special emphasis on conserving "greenbelts"— natural corridors that link larger parcels of land. Greenbelt acquires and conserves land by gift or purchase, through perpetual conservation restrictions, and by facilitating land conservation projects in collaborative partnerships. With a small staff and an army of dedicated volunteers, and through generous contributions, we have conserved over 10,000 acres of important land throughout Essex County.

Essex County contains salt marshes, rolling hills, serene forests, rich streams, and rocky shores. We treasure this open space as a critical component of our cultural heritage, our economic vitality, and our quality of life. As the only organization working exclusively to conserve land throughout the Essex County region, Greenbelt fosters intimate knowledge of the region's special lands, so we can effectively conserve them. Greenbelt's presence can be felt in communities throughout the county, where we work cooperatively with landowners, local government, businesses, and other organizations to implement land protection projects.

Land acquired by Greenbelt is not only protected in perpetuity, but stewarded to conserve its ecological, scenic, or agricultural value. Our land stewardship staff is out on the properties nearly every day, maintaining trails, monitoring plant and animal species, and restoring habitat for wildlife. All of this work ensures that humans and wildlife will enjoy these lands for generations to come.

We invite you to explore the wonder of Essex County, which hosts several rare plant and animal species and has been visited by more than half, or about 400, of all the species of birds known in North America. *The Guidebook* will lead you through some of the best little-known wildlife areas, and invites you to walk, hike, kayak, canoe, fish, study plants and birds, or simply bring a picnic and a book to relax at one of our many spectacular properties. Greenbelt properties are open to the public free of charge every day from sunrise to sunset.

Greenbelt offers a variety of programs for the community. We invite members and the public to join our regularly scheduled monthly walks to learn about the ecology, wildlife, and rich natural and human history of the area. Our Speakers Bureau program offers an introduction to Greenbelt's mission and accomplishments, highlights the critical need for open space conservation in Essex County, and features spectacular photographs of our region. Greenbelt's education committee has designed three curriculum guides to help teachers and students get out on our properties and learn in the best way possible–by digging into the earth and discovering science and nature themselves. Greenbelt hosts family events at the Cox Reservation headquarters, such as Fall Festival, a day of apple-picking and cider-pressing at our own orchard; Art in the Barn, one of the premier art exhibits of the region; and other activities throughout the year.

Ultimately, Greenbelt depends on you to continue this important work. Please join your many neighbors who support Greenbelt as members and volunteers. Membership with Greenbelt offers many benefits, the greatest of which is the satisfaction of knowing you are helping to conserve important land today and for the future.

For more information about Greenbelt, or to join us as a member or volunteer, visit our website at www.ecga.org, or contact us at (978) 768-7241 or ecga@ecga.org. A membership enrollment form is included at the back of *The Guidebook*.

USING THE GREENBELT GUIDEBOOK

The Guidebook highlights some of the best hikes, river trips and natural history of Essex County Greenbelt Association properties. Properties are listed in alphabetical order, and guided walks and easy-to-use maps will help you locate and navigate each property. Symbols located above each property heading indicate visitor activities for each site.

           = Hiking

           = Birding and Nature Study

           = Fishing

           = Canoeing and Kayaking

           = Snowshoeing and Cross-Country Skiing

A Nature Calendar, which you will find in the back-cover pocket of *The Guidebook*, offers suggestions for selecting a walk according to the time of year, and describes some of the interesting mammals, birds, amphibians, flowers, and trees which appear seasonally on particular properties.

While visiting the properties described in *The Guidebook*, please be thoughtful, and follow these few guidelines:

• Visit between sunrise and sunset only.
• Carry out what you carry in.
• Do not park in front of gates, or otherwise block main entrances. This is often the only avenue available for emergency vehicles.
• Keep to the perimeter of hayfields, and do not walk through them. Greenbelt hayfields often contain fragile ground-nests of grassland birds, or are reserved for agricultural production.

Dog owners are asked to follow these guidelines:
- Carry a leash.
- Leash aggressive dogs.
- Do not leave dogs unattended.
- Control excessive noise.
- Pick up and dispose of dog waste.
- Prevent digging and destructive behavior.

The following activities are not permitted on the properties:
- Lighting of fires.
- Disposing of trash.
- Use of motorized vehicles.
- Target shooting.
- Hunting without permission.
- Trespassing from sunset to sunrise.

In the case of horseback riding or mountain biking, please do not ride on trails during that time when frost is leaving the ground in early spring, or other times when trails are very muddy.

As a visitor to our properties, you can help us with land stewardship by reporting areas which need attention, as well as unusual plants, birds, mammals, reptiles or amphibians you observe for inclusion in our inventory of native inhabitants. We have designed this *Guidebook* to fit into your pocket so that you can carry it in your travels. Enjoy your time in the natural world!

THE LANDSCAPE OF ESSEX COUNTY

Formation of the Landscape

Essex County, covering approximately 500 square miles in northeastern Massachusetts, is characterized by its rocky coastlines and sandy beaches, salt and fresh water marshes, river valleys and rolling hills, fallow and cultivated fields, and deciduous, mixed and coniferous forests. Virtually all of the major northeastern habitat types, except mountains, can be found in the county, which lies in a climatic and biological transition zone between the northerly Canadian Zone and the southerly Austral Zone. Climate, geology, and over 9,000 years of human occupation have played key roles in shaping the modern day flora, fauna and scenery found across this unique and beautiful county.

Perhaps more than any other event, glaciation literally shaped the Essex County landscape. For much of the past 3 million years, the county was covered with ice, most recently by the Laurentide Ice Cap, which scraped and polished the landscape as it slowly pushed southward. The eventual melting, which began about 13,000 years ago and lasted about 2000 years, left behind the hills, valleys and eroded materials that make up today's landscape.

Today as we travel Essex County, evidence of this glaciation is all around us: small glacial lakes, kettle holes, erratic boulders, sand dunes, till moraines, and drumlins (see glossary for definitions). The glaciers scoured the earth, pushing aside rock and sand, and as they melted, much of this material was deposited along our coast. The melted ice, just as the glaciers had before them, flowed from north to south creating the rivers, valleys and watersheds of today. Many of the current coastal harbors are actually "drowned valleys" – eroded coastal valleys that filled with saltwater as the sea level rose.

Glacial melting also caused the land to rise, as it was released from the great weight and pressure of the glaciers. The shifting earth pushed up in many places, creating hills and deepening valleys. The ensuing hundreds and thousands of years brought continued erosion of the hills and valleys from rainfall and snow melt, bringing a constant source of new loose material to the coastline. This has resulted in Essex County's ever-changing shoreline, where barrier beaches and sand dunes are constantly shifting and adjusting to the new sediments brought down the rivers and pushed about by the ocean's waves and currents.

Current inhabitants or visitors to Essex County view the landscape at a fixed point in time. From one year to the next, changes are subtle and slow. The geological formations found here are awesome. They are the foundation of the landscape. But equally fascinating is the impact that human occupation, both ancient and more recent, has had on the natural history and landscape of the county.

Native American Habitation

The retreat of the glaciers left behind a frozen and barren landscape. The first flora to return were grasses, which eventually developed into grassy plains, and attracted some of the early megafauna such as 300-pound beavers, gigantic short-faced bears and the woolly mammoth. As the landscape and flora continued to develop, these original creatures disappeared due to their inability to adapt to changing landscape and climatic conditions. Eventually a more forested landscape created additional habitats and natural resources that would play a significant role in the natural and human history of Essex County.

Native Americans are believed to be the first humans to occupy post-glacial Essex County approximately 9,000 years ago. Practicing a yearly cycle of seasonal migration, Native American peoples wintered in inland locations in small family groups; congregated at river sites in the spring to catch and smoke anadromous alewife and herring fish; then moved to coastal areas during the summer, to harvest and store plentiful marine resources such as fish, shellfish, waterfowl, and shorebirds. The summer months also afforded many wild edible plants such as wild rice, nuts, seeds, grapes, and berries, and Native Americans cultivated a few low-maintenance crops such as corn, squash, beans, and Jerusalem artichoke. The first New Englanders hunted moose, bear, deer, elk, and small game in the fall, and in the winter supplemented fresh meat with dried food supplies harvested during other seasons.

Native American peoples established encampment sites at the mouth of the Merrimack River, on Plum Island, and on Castle Neck. At least 100 Native American dwelling or burial sites have been discovered in Haverhill, Saugus, Georgetown and Andover, and over 200 encampment sites have been identified on Cape Ann.

The land management technique used most frequently by Native Americans was fire. Through periodic burning, the people kept forests passable, cleared shooting lanes for hunting game, caused natural selection of hardwood nut-producing trees such as oak, chestnut, and hickory, and promoted the growth of berry-producing plants such as blueberries and huckleberries. This abundance of nuts and berries, along with grassy forest floors, provided abundant food for game species. A mix of field and open understory forest dominated the inland landscape and constituted rich wildlife habitat.

Native Americans lived for thousands of years in Essex County, managing the land to promote food sources for humans and wildlife, and otherwise minimizing human impact through nomadic, subsistence-based land use patterns. It was not until Europeans arrived in the seventeenth century that rapid change began to take place in the landscape.

European Settlement

European colonists had a dramatic impact on the landscape of Essex County. Arriving on the shores of Massachusetts from countries where natural resources had been under pressure for centuries, the early European settlers discovered an abundance of fish, wildlife, and trees beyond their wildest dreams. Early accounts of the landscape often describe it in terms of commodities, such as fur-bearing animals, fowl, fish and trees. These same resources that were bountiful for Native Americans attracted ever-increasing numbers of Europeans, who quickly established new colonies. Essex County was settled in the early 1600's as the colonists found protected coastal waters in the many harbors and salt marshes. In the first decades of settlement, the Europeans acquired many skills from the Native Americans, which allowed them to successfully harvest natural resources and adapt to the New England landscape. Between 1640 and 1800, records indicate that Essex County was the most densely populated area in all of New England.

Stories abound extolling the richness and abundance of natural resources in Essex County. Reports describe oysters a foot long and oyster banks a mile long. Shorebirds and ducks were so abundant in the salt marshes that colonists bragged of killing "50 at a shot." Striped bass were so plentiful in coastal waters that colonists were eventually prohibited from using them as fertilizer in their fields in an effort to protect their populations. This restriction may have been the very first conservation law of its type passed in Massachusetts. Abundant inshore and offshore fish populations, combined with a ready overseas market in Europe, spurred the development of a commercial fishing industry. This fishing industry, along with its subsidiary shipbuilding industry, took a predominant place alongside local agriculture as a staple of the Essex County economy.

Tremendous change occurred on many levels as a result of this fast growing, agricultural and fisheries-based economy. Land was systematically cleared for farmland, lumber, and fuel. Cities and towns were founded across the county. Native American populations decreased rapidly as a result of warfare with the new settlers over land ownership and access rights, but more significantly from diseases such as chicken pox and small pox, for which they had no natural resistance. Entire Native American villages were wiped out, a tragic end for many dignified and courageous people who knew how to live with the land. Historical accounts through town records and other sources tell a story about changing landscape which includes deforestation, agriculture and the extermination of predators that were believed to threaten livestock. Studies to clarify the landscape history of the colonial years continue today, using techniques such as tree ring identification, pollen layers in bogs, and archeology.

The advent of the industrial revolution brought with it a new era in landscape history. During the 1700 and 1800's, the expanding population of Essex County relied heavily on natural resources to drive the economy. Forests continued to be cleared for lumber and many rivers were dammed to generate power for manufacturing. Deforestation produced wide-scale change in habitat, which resulted in rapid change in species composition of many plants and animals throughout the county. Pollution from human waste and manufacturing byproducts altered rivers, lakes, and coastal waters. The overall result was a degradation of environmental quality in many areas, particularly in densely populated centers like Lawrence, Salem and Gloucester. Burgeoning populations and growing economies decimated much of the flora and fauna that had initially lured Europeans to the continent. Then, with the advent of mechanized farming and the railroad, it became clear that the small patches of hilly boulder-strewn and irregularly shaped parcels of land in Essex County could not be cultivated as efficiently as the large, flat tracts of land in the Midwest, and local agriculture was gradually abandoned.

Modern Day Landscape

The local economic needs of Essex County inhabitants have always shaped the landscape. The Native American subsistence-based economy prompted inhabitants to manage the land through periodic burning to produce open woodlands full of hardwoods, berries, and abundant wildlife as food sources. The agricultural and fisheries-based economy of the European colonists led these inhabitants to clear farmland, while the later manufacturing-based economy led inhabitants in the 1800's and early 1900's to harness the power of rivers to convert raw materials to manufactured goods and to abandon active farming on land which their ancestors had worked so hard to clear. Much of the open farmland and pastureland gave way to forest succession, and became woodlands once again. In the latter part of the 20th century, several economic factors impacted Essex County and the corresponding demands placed upon the landscape. The once abundant natural resources such as the George's Bank fishery became depleted; globalization of the economy has lured manufacturers to other regions and countries in search of natural resources and inexpensive labor; and the economy has shifted to a service and information-based economy. In the current "Information Age," land is most highly valued for residential and commercial development.

While much of the landscape is once again wooded, large unbroken tracts are rarer now than ever before. Habitat fragmentation occurs at a tremendous rate as the human population in the county grows, and results in the decline of those species of plants, birds, and animals that require unbroken habitat. Some species have gone through dramatic cycles or have been drastically altered, while others have disappeared forever. Passenger Pigeons, Great Auks, Heath Hens, and Eskimo Curlews, once found in awesome abundance in our skies and along our shores, are now extinct everywhere. Bears, wolves, and mountain lions were eliminated from the county through predator control by farmers concerned for their livestock. Both popular game species, elk and wild turkey were extirpated from Essex County prior to the advent of regulated harvesting and management of wildlife in the 1930's and 1940's. Beavers, fishers, and coyotes have returned in the wake of 19th and 20th century decline of agriculture and subsequent reforestation. Wild turkeys have since been reintroduced in the past few decades using stock from New York, and now roam the forests and fields once again. Elk have not returned to Essex County due to habitat fragmentation. Exotic flora and fauna from other continents have been introduced to the area inadvertently through imported agricultural materials, as ornamental plants, or as attempts at biological control of other pests, and now compete for habitat in many areas, overtaking and displacing native species. English house sparrows, European buckthorn, bittersweet, honeysuckle, Japanese knotweed, and purple loosestrife are classic examples of invasive exotic species which have displaced native species and now flourish in Essex County.

Water is always a precious commodity in any area, and today watershed protection and enhancement is an important effort in Essex County. Runoff from storm water collects many contaminants as it flows into local streams and rivers, and eventually makes its way into coastal waters. These contaminants can adversely affect many species of flora and fauna found locally. Greater awareness on the part of communities and citizens in Essex County is helping to reduce the amount of this non-point source pollution. (For more information about watershed protection, contact the Ipswich River Watershed Association at 978-356-0418 or www.ipswichriver.org, or the Parker River Clean Water Association at 978-462-2551 or www.parker-river.org.)

When we travel Essex County today, we can still see the breath-taking beauty and many of the abundant natural resources that sustained Native Americans and greeted early European settlers. It is a living landscape that tells the story of millennia and centuries of change through glaciation and geological processes, changing species composition, dammed rivers and mill sites, abandoned granite quarries and overgrown farmlands, and the varied human populations that have inhabited and utilized the land and sea. We can learn about the human and natural history of the landscape by studying geology, history, ecology, botany, and by learning to read features such as cellar holes, stone walls, old stumps, composition of plant communities and other clues that we find while out in the landscape. (For more information, see *Reading the Forested Landscape* by Tom Wessels.)

Now you have a special opportunity to travel Essex County, using this *Guidebook* to visit Essex County Greenbelt Association properties and experience this wonderful landscape firsthand. For over 40 years we have been conserving land to perpetuate the ecological, agricultural, and scenic value of Essex County. We invite you to visit, explore, and enjoy each and every property. We hope you will develop your own knowledge and appreciation of the special habitats and views conserved in perpetuity and described in these pages. The landscape story will continue over time, but our work of conserving the landscape of Essex County is far from completed. We hope that you will join with us at the Essex County Greenbelt Association, so that we all might have access to places where streams flow freely, trees grow tall, and wildlife can flourish forever.

Yellow Bellied
Sapsucker

21

Dorothy Kerper Monnelly

Alt Woodland — Beverly

Directions:

From Route 128: Take Exit 18 to Route 22 north toward Essex and Wenham. Follow Route 22 north 0.5 mile and turn left onto Grover Street. Proceed 0.5 mile on Grover Street. The entrance is on the left, immediately after Gavin Circle.

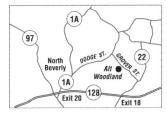

From the North Beverly Train Station: Travel down Dodge Street 1.4 miles, and turn right onto Grover Street. Follow Grover 0.6 mile to the entrance on the right.

From the Montserrat Train Station: Take Route 22 East towards Hamilton for 1.7 miles, then turn left onto Grover Street. Follow Grover 0.5 mile to the entrance on the left.

Parking: The parking area is marked with a Greenbelt sign and metal gate. Please do not block the gate, and park parallel to the road. Parking is limited to two cars.

General Description:

Alt Woodland encompasses 61 acres. The property is a patchwork of former pastures that have been allowed to grow since the early 1900's. The shallow soil of this property, which falls into the "Chatfield" soil family, has determined both the type of plants which can grow here and the human uses of the property. The lack of soil depth discourages the growth of hardwood trees such as maple, which require an adequate supply of water and prefer deeper soils for stability. However, white pine has thrived in the soil of the Alt Woodland, since it can grow in

Dragon's Mouth Orchid

arid sites and establish a root system capable of anchoring to large rocks. The shallow soil of this property makes it impossible to dig a hole for a privy or root cellar. Therefore, it is no surprise that remnants of past habitation do not exist here. Greenbelt currently manages this forest for timber, with the goals of enhancing wildlife populations and providing visitors a peaceful place to walk among the pines.

Special Features:

In April or May, you may hear or catch a glimpse of a Pine Warbler, Hermit Thrush, or Rufous-sided Towhee. Pileated Woodpeckers, Red-tailed Hawks, Great Horned Owls, fox, and deer may be seen during any season. Beaver Pond is a relic white cedar swamp and an historic site for *Arethusa bulbosa*, or Dragon's Mouth. This rare member of the Orchid family is 5-10" high and has a magenta-pink flower, 1" long, with the lower lip purple-spotted and crested with yellow hairs. After the plant blooms, a grasslike leaf develops. We'll give a reward for the rediscovery of this plant. Provide us with a photograph of the flower in situ. Please do not pick! Special geologic features of this property include Cape Ann granite, esker, and glacial outwash.

A Walk:

Enter at the gate and walk down the old woods road. Take your second right, which is another woods road running along the right edge of a clearing. As you follow this road through the hilly contours of these upland woods, look for signs of this land's history of poor soils, logging and fire. Lowbush blueberry, American beech, and black huckleberry are all woody indicator plants for these conditions. Similarly, bracken fern, haircap moss and partridgeberry are non-woody indicators. As you descend toward the bottom of the hill, notice that some of these plants fade away, while others, such as speckled alder, birch, and red-osier dogwood, take their place.

Take the trail on the left at the bottom of the hill, go over a bridge, through a stone wall, and left on another old road. Follow the trail until you reach a left turn where the old road bridges a wet area. If you are feeling botanically adventurous, you may bushwhack to Beaver Pond to look for Arethusa, following an intermittent water course which feeds the pond. Otherwise, turn left over the bridge, continue up the hill, through a stone wall, and right at the top of the hill. Take this trail back to main woods road, on which you'll turn left to head back to the gate.

FIELD NOTES

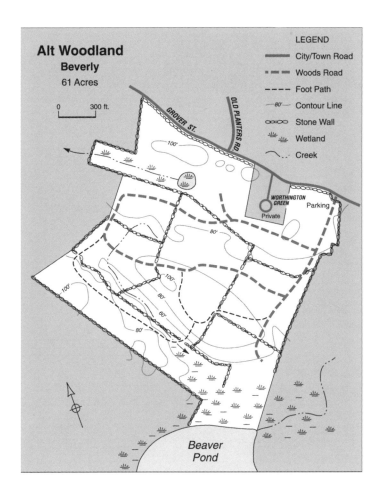

Dorothy Kerper Monnelly

Bald Hill East — Boxford

Directions:

From East Boxford Center: Travel one block north on Georgetown Road, and turn left onto Middleton Road. At the next intersection, just past the school, continue straight, then proceed about 0.7 mile to a small pullout just after a small white house on the right.

From Route 95: Take the Endicott Street, Boxford exit. Head west from the exit ramp for 0.2 mile. Turn north onto Middleton Road and travel 2.4 miles to the pullout on the left by a small white house.

Parking: Park in the pullout next to the white house, by the Phillips Wildlife Sanctuary sign. Parking is limited to two cars. Note: This is the site marked "Bald Hill East Parking" on the property map and not the larger "Crooked Pond Parking" area about half a mile to the south.

General Description:

Greenbelt protects 20 parcels, with a total of 386 acres, within a much larger protected area. Bald Hill East is adjacent to Boxford State Forest's Longmeadow Swamp and the John Phillips Wildlife Sanctuary, which together consist of 1,800 acres of large land tracts spread across the towns of Boxford, North Andover, and Middleton. Here we highlight the Greenbelt inholdings, representing some of Greenbelt's earliest acquisitions.

Special Features:

The Bald Hill area is one of Essex County's best assemblages of rich forest land, diverse wetlands, and associated biological diversity that you are likely to visit. Springtime wildflowers, migratory birds, and vernal pools; summertime sedges and breeding raptors; and fall foliage and winter tracking make this property worth a visit any time of the year. Geologic features include Boxford Nashoba Formation, Fish Brook gneiss, quartz hornblende diorite, drumlin, and glacial outwash.

A more detailed trail map of the area, available at the Greenbelt office, shows the numbered trail intersections, and allows the visitor to comfortably navigate the maze of trails and plan a half-hour visit or an all-day trek. The features most often visited are Crooked Pond and the slopes of Bald Hill. This is one of the best areas for hard-to-find breeding birds in the county, including Louisiana Waterthrushes, Winter Wrens, Yellow-throated Vireos, Pileated Woodpeckers, Red-shouldered Hawks, and Northern Goshawks. In spring you will almost certainly run into birders near Crooked Pond. Other rewarding areas for study are the sections in or near Greenbelt's Haynes Woodlot and Ox Pastures. This is a favorite location for viewing wildflowers blooming in April and May. This huge forest is also an excellent place to see fishers.

Barred Owl

30

A Walk:

The walk starts at the small pullout and will take you through four different Greenbelt parcels. The full walk will take approximately 2 to 2 1/2 hours, and possibly more if you take time along the way for nature study. As you start up the path, the white house will be on your right. Just beyond the house, the path branches at marker #20A; take the right branch, which runs straight ahead. The woods on either side of you now are quite different from each other. On your left is a deciduous forest of white, red and black oaks. On your right, as you walk up the path, is a mixed coniferous/deciduous forest consisting of pines, birches, and shagbark hickories.

Longmeadow

Farther along the path, you will approach a culvert and wooded wetland on your right. The culvert is one of the outlets to Longmeadow, our 8-acre reservation, which was donated by Greenbelt founder Dr. Stephen Maddock. The wooded wetland is at the foot of a north-facing, hemlock-covered slope and is one of the last ponds in the county to thaw in spring, retaining ice far longer than most other woodland ponds. The swamp there is a sure-fire place to hear the amazing song of the Winter Wren in spring, while the hemlock grove is often home to a pair of Barred Owls. About 100 yards from the culvert, the path turns sharply away from the meadow and climbs to intersection #21. The trail to the left leads to our Haynes Woodlot, to which we will later return. But now, take the trail to the right, and you will find Ox and Peabody pastures, with their large banks of woodland wildflowers.

Ox Pasture

The entrance to Ox Pasture is on your right; it is the only trail intersection on this trail without a number. This 14-acre pasture was also donated by Dr. Maddock. You will enter through a cut in the stone wall. Watch for Ruffed Grouse often seen in this open woodland. The path leads to a knoll which, during winter months, affords a view of Longmeadow below. You can find a number of open-form shrubs along this path, including witch hazel, the only native shrub to bloom in the fall.

Retrace your steps now from the knoll at Ox Pasture back to the main path where you turned in. Turn right, then to continue with the full 2 to 2 1/2 hour walk, bear right at the next fork labeled intersection #26, and the path will lead you through Peabody Pasture. (The marker for intersection #26 is a wooden marker, about eight feet high on a tree, whereas the majority of trail markers in the area are attached to brown fiberglass stakes.)

Alternately, if you wish a shorter walk, turn left at intersection #26 and follow the trail to intersection #13 at Crooked Pond. Along this section of trail, you will note some flooding of woodlands due to beaver activity. Look for Pileated Woodpeckers, Northern Flickers, and other cavity-nesting birds in dead, standing trees. Continue following directions for your guided walk under "Crooked Pond" below.

Peabody Pasture
Peabody Pasture is a 20-acre woodland donated by Henry Sawyer of Middleton, another of Greenbelt's founders. This pasture is in the later stages of forest succession, and may be difficult to discern from the neighboring woodlands. Look for subtle clues in the landscape to see if you can detect its historical use. Common juniper is one species indicative of old pastureland. You may spot only remnants of this sun-loving shrub, which has succumbed to a forest overstory.

Bald Hill
As you continue on the trail, you may see remnants of an old trail on your left, which previously led to the top of Bald Hill, but was discontinued years ago in order to provide undisturbed habitat for nesting Northern Goshawks. Continue around the base of Bald Hill to intersection 8A and turn left. You will pass by a right hand turn at

intersection #9 and then at the next possible left hand turn, turn left to climb Bald Hill. At the first major intersection (#27), turn left and climb until you reach a clearing. Bear left to follow the edges of the clearing and explore the top of Bald Hill, Greenbelt's first protected property and part of the Boxford State Forest. Return to intersection #27 and take the trail opposite from the summit to descend Bald Hill. Then at intersection #12, turn left, and pass through intersection #13A to #13.

Crooked Pond
At intersection #13, turn right if you have come from the summit of Bald Hill, or turn left if you have taken the shorter loop from Ox Pasture. You will see Crooked Pond on your right, which is a prime spot for birding. At intersection #14, turn left, and bear left again at intersection #23. Bear right at intersection #22, and just beyond it, you will come to a vernal pool that marks the most northwesterly corner of the Haynes Woodlot.

Haynes Woodlot
This woodlot was donated by Winthrop Haynes, an early Greenbelt member, and his family. It is a fabulous place to study flowers and salamanders. The established path does not go through this property but skirts its northern boundary, which is marked by a stone wall. Follow the path to the base of a hill and continue to intersection #20A, near the white cottage. You are now about 200 feet from the road and your car.

FIELD NOTES

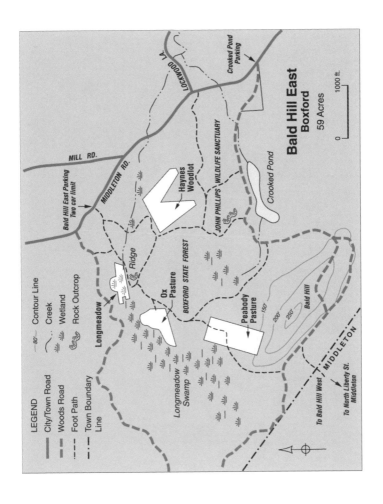

Bald Hill East
Boxford
59 Acres

LEGEND

City/Town Road
Woods Road
Foot Path
Town Boundary Line

—80— Contour Line
Creek
Wetland
Rock Outcrop

0   1000 ft.

LOCKWOOD

Crooked Pond Parking

MILL RD.

MIDDLETON RD.

Bald Hill East Parking
Two car limit

Haynes Woodlot

JOHN PHILLIPS WILDLIFE SANCTUARY

Crooked Pond

Ridge

Ox Pasture

Longmeadow

BOXFORD STATE FOREST

Peabody Pasture

150'

200'

250'

Bald Hill

Longmeadow Swamp

MIDDLETON

To Bald Hill West

To North Liberty St. Middleton

Dorothy Kerper Monnelly

Bald Hill West — Middleton

Directions:
From the Danvers intersection of Routes 1 and 62: Head west 2.0 miles on Route 62 into Middleton. Turn right onto Liberty Street. Drive 2.5 miles on Liberty Street to where the pavement ends. The entrance is another 0.2 mile down the dirt road, on the right where three walls converge on a lane and a pipe gate bars the way. Be sure the gate is closed after you pass through; cows are pastured on this property.

Parking: Parking is limited to two cars. Park parallel to the road.

General Description:
Bald Hill West consists of 222 acres, composed of six separate gifts of land near the Boxford town line. The Captain Bill and Pine Hill lots came from Henry Sawyer of Middleton, the Prichard and Esty Woodlots from Charles Prichard, the Jopp Lot from Sally Curtis, formerly of Topsfield, and the Clapp Woodlot from Helen Clapp. If you are unfamiliar with this area, we suggest you carry along a compass and the USGS South Groveland, Georgetown and Reading topographic maps. This *Guidebook* map represents only a small corner of a large forested tract of land owned by the state, Greenbelt, and other private entities. Other maps of the area include the Bald Hill Reservation Map (showing the entire area and trail intersection numbers, available at the Greenbelt office) and a contour and vegetation cover map published by the New England Orienteering

Club (www.newenglandorienteering.org/maps.htm.) It would be wise to familiarize yourself with a particular woodlot on each visit, and build on experience by exploring new lots later on, thus developing a thorough knowledge of the entire area.

From a natural history perspective, this area is a mosaic of habitats which support an extraordinary diversity of plant and animal life. The bedrock in this area, hornblende diorite and hornblende epidote gneiss, provides a higher pH for the soils than the typical granite of Essex County. Columbine, hepatica, bloodroot, pink lady's slipper, maidenhair fern and ebony spleenwort, all plants that thrive on sweeter soils, can be found on the rocky talus slopes here. The landscape has also been shaped by its past use as woodlot and pasture; remnants of the pasture and stone walls still exist today and you may find them hidden within the new-growth forest. Fire has been another influence on this land. In March 2000, a mild spring fire that swept through nearly sixty acres of the woods cleared away the forest litter and killed young white pines, but left the larger hardwoods undamaged. Wetlands, ponds, and at least two dozen vernal pools add another layer of diversity to this area, and in recent years beavers have been very active here, creating even more wetlands. The mosquitoes can be ferocious: long pants and sleeves, and a hat with a head net are recommended for spring and summer hiking. Despite mosquitoes, a walk during the months of May and June is well worthwhile, as

Clethra alnifolia
Sweet Pepperbush

38

wildflowers are in their glory and the migrating and courting birds are most noticeable and active.

Special Features:

The Bald Hill West Reservation offers an excellent place to study mammals. Acting as the westerly gate to the Boxford State Forest, these woodlots are part of a much larger wildlife refuge. In the winter months, it is rewarding to don snowshoes or cross county skis and head out across the woods. The snow becomes the record book for all the scurrying and tramping of the local fauna. In these woods, one can study the tracks of the white-tailed deer, coyote, red fox, fisher, mink, otter, weasel, raccoon, skunk, cottontail rabbit, red squirrel, grey squirrel, flying squirrel, meadow vole, short-tailed shrew and white-footed mouse. Even an occasional moose may wander into the area. Other mammals exist here but may not be active in winter, or may be subterranean in habit. There is no doubt that they are there; you simply have to discover them. Some useful tracking guides include the *Peterson Field Guide to Animal Tracks*, and *Tracking and The Art of Seeing* by Paul Rezendes.

A Walk:

Since this is such a large network of trails, there are nearly limitless combinations for exploration. Below are a few suggestions for interesting and enjoyable walks.

1) Prichard Woodlot Exploration: 1.7 miles. From the entrance at Liberty Street, go through the gate (making sure it is closed behind you), and along the trail which veers off toward the left. This area is a thicket of multiflora rose and barberry, both exotic invasive plants, and may sometimes be a little overgrown. This first stretch is also private property, so please respect our neighbor and any of his cows you may encounter. The trail will cross a brook which drains from Sharpners Pond and Pout Pond to Boston Brook, and eventually to

the Ipswich River. In the early spring, marsh marigold can be seen here; in the summer, cardinal flower. Just beyond the brook is the Greenbelt gate and boundary. The fire mentioned above started near here and spread uphill and on both sides of the trail for about 200 yards. See if you can detect any signs of the fire: scorched tree trunks or differences in the forest vegetation. For an easy hike where you don't have to think about navigation, stay on the main trail. It will wind through dry upland forests of blueberry, red oak, hickory and white pine, and then down into wet areas with boardwalks, vernal pools, ferns, sedges, and skunk cabbage. Thrushes and warblers seem to enjoy this area, and a walk in May or June should be rich with the songs of Veery, American Robin, Ovenbird, and Louisiana Waterthrush. Spring peepers, wood frogs, American toads, and bullfrogs sing from the wetlands and vernal pools from early spring through summer. When the trail crosses a stone wall and trees marked with blue blazes, you'll be leaving the Prichard Woodlot and entering the Boxford State Forest. This main trail meets up with the Bald Hill trail at intersection #9. Turn around and retrace your steps to get back to your car.

2) Pout Pond Bushwhack: 1.5 miles. For the more adventurous, or if you're in the mood to test your map and compass skills, try to find Pout Pond. About 1/3 of a mile in from the gate, veer off to the left on a side trail for a bit, and then head in a northerly direction for about 1/4 mile. Deer trails will be quite evident, especially in winter, and may lead you to the pond. Once there, you will be rewarded with the sight of a place that seems as though it has been untouched by humans. White cedar grows thickly around the edges of the pond, and red maple provides a splash of color in the early autumn. *Myrica gale*, leatherleaf, and other bog plants also grow around the margin. Recent beaver activity in the area may eventually change the ecology of this wetland, killing the white cedars as the water level rises. This is a good winter trip, as ice will allow you access to areas that are nearly impassable during summer.

3) Mill Street Two-car Option: 3 miles. Follow the driving directions as described above, but after 1.3 miles on Liberty Street, turn right onto Peabody Street. After 0.4 mile, turn left onto Mill Street. You'll go over Boston Brook, and then veer left, following the road all the way to the end of the cul-de-sac. A dirt lane will exit the cul-de-sac to the right after the very last house; follow it until you reach a pull-off and woods road that goes to the right. Leave one of your cars here, making sure you do not block either the dirt lane or the woods road. Drive to the Prichard Woodlot Liberty Street entrance and leave your second car. Follow the Prichard Woodlot exploration walk as described above. At trail marker #9, turn right and walk along the base of Bald Hill. At trail marker #10, take the trail on the right. This old road, shown as "Thomas Road" on the Bald Hill map, historically led down to where Peabody Street meets the Ipswich River. Along this stretch, it will lead you past an old cemetery and the remains of a house on your left. After passing the cemetery, the main trail will cross a stone wall, and make an almost right angle turn, skirting some wetlands. About 200 yards after the turn, a smaller trail will diverge from the Thomas Road trail, and head off to the right. This trail will lead you through our Esty, Hatfield, and Jopp Woodlots, back to the Mill Road extension.

FIELD NOTES

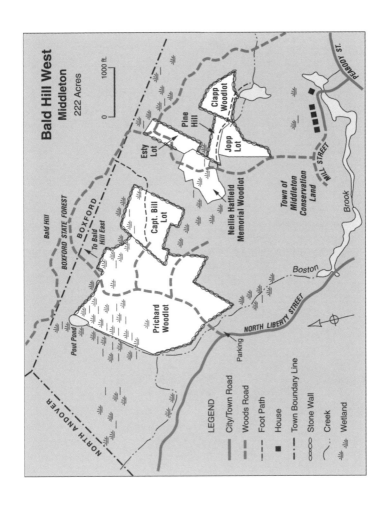

Bald Hill West
Middleton
222 Acres

1000 ft.

Bald Hill

BOXFORD STATE FOREST

BOXFORD

To Bald Hill East

Clapp Woodlot

Pine Hill

Jopp Lot

Esty Lot

Nellie Hatfield Memorial Woodlot

Capt. Bill Lot

Town of Middleton Conservation Land

Brook

PEABODY ST.

MILL STREET

Boston

Prichard Woodlot

Pout Pond

NORTH LIBERTY STREET

Parking

NORTH ANDOVER

LEGEND

City/Town Road
Woods Road
Foot Path
House
Town Boundary Line
Stone Wall
Creek
Wetland

Dorothy Kerper Monnelly

Baldpate Hill — Georgetown

Directions:

From Route 95: Take Exit 54 onto Route 133 west toward Georgetown. Follow Route 133 through Georgetown center for another 0.8 mile and turn left onto Baldpate Road. Proceed 1.0 mile on Baldpate Road to a dirt access road on the right.

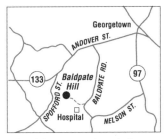

Parking: Park on the right shoulder of Baldpate Road and do not block the cable gate. Parking is limited to six cars.

General Description:

Greenbelt land on Baldpate Hill consists of 17 acres, which surrounds the fire tower at the top of the dirt road. The property is near Baldpate Pond and a satellite Massachusetts Division of Forest and Parks property. If you were to continue down Baldpate Road toward Boxford, these sites would be on the left.

This Greenbelt property sits on top of one of Essex County's drumlins. Most of the rounded hills in the county are drumlins and are the result of glacial action. The process of formation is not entirely understood. One depiction of the process is to visualize a large stubborn lump of clay, which has been pushed down into the bedrock by an advancing glacier. You will notice on a topographic map that all the drumlins in this area have an orientation in a northwest/southeast direction. This demonstrates the course of the advancing glacier some twelve thousand years ago.

45

Baldpate Hill has been identified by the Early Sites Research Society as a potential Native American ceremonial site. Fire rings have been discovered near the summit. The nearby Chaplin property provided the large white oaks harvested for the original planking of *U.S.S. Constitution*. The trees grew on the protected southwest side of this drumlin, and were thus sheltered from the northeasterly gales. The strength of this wood gave the ship its nickname "Old Ironsides." The fire tower perched atop the hill was built in 1913, and demonstrates the government's campaign to stamp out forest fires; it is still in use today. We now know that many native wild species depend upon fire clearings in the forest. For example, two upland game birds, the Ruffed Grouse and American Woodcock, require large openings in the forest canopy for the regeneration of their preferred habitat and to perform courtship displays. These openings were originally

Ruby Meadowhawk
Dragonfly

46

created by wind and fire and later by man's wood cutting. But in the last century, the regeneration of eastern forests has reduced the number and size of canopy openings. Consequently, Ruffed Grouse and American Woodcock populations have declined throughout Essex County.

Special Features:

Scarlet Tanagers, House Wrens, and ruby meadowhawk dragonflies can be spotted in summer, and gray tree frogs can be heard calling, especially after rain. Historically, Ruffed Grouse lived here; it's up to the visitor to determine if they still do. On the walk up the hill, you may catch the scent of ripening grapes in September. Look for the black locust grove near the water tanks. Baldpate Hill's distinguishing geologic feature is that it is a drumlin.

A Walk:

The steep ascent of the access road offers an opportunity to work up a good sweat. Once at the top of the hill, the property does not have trails and is a good place for honing your land navigation skills. Take a topographic map and a compass, and see if you can find a particular corner of the property by setting a course. It is not possible to get lost, since the property is totally surrounded by stone walls. The Massachusetts Division of Fisheries and Wildlife offers a free introductory course on Map, Compass and Survival Skills. Visit their website at: www.masswildlife.org or call (508) 792-7434 for more information.

FIELD NOTES

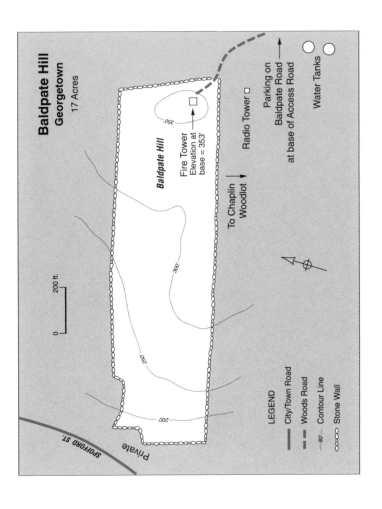

Baldpate Hill
Georgetown
17 Acres

Baldpate Hill

Fire Tower
Elevation at
base = 353'

350

300

250

200

To Chaplin
Woodlot

Radio Tower □

Parking on
Baldpate Road
at base of Access Road

Water Tanks

SPOFFORD ST.

Private

0   200 ft.

LEGEND
City/Town Road
Woods Road
—80'— Contour Line
Stone Wall

49

Dorothy Kerper Monnelly

Beverly Conservation Area — Beverly

Directions:

From Route 128: Take Exit 17 and turn south on Grapevine Road toward Beverly Farms. Follow Grapevine Road 1.5 miles to Chapman's Nursery on the right. Turn right just before the nursery onto Greenwood Avenue, and proceed to the point where Greenwood Avenue ends at a cable gate and Stone Ridge Road heads off to the right.

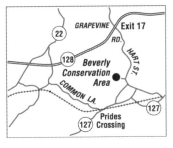

Parking: Park to the right on Stone Ridge Road. Please do not block the gate.

General Description:

Greenbelt owned property within the larger Beverly Conservation Area consists of 126 acres. The area has long been referred to as Beverly Commons, and during colonial times was a major thoroughfare from Salem to Gloucester, an important source of firewood as woodlots, and later, a common pasture area for grazing sheep. The area was also historically known as "The Witches' Wood," since a number of colonial families took up temporary residence here, fleeing from the Salem witchcraft hysteria of 1692. This woodland is a rare asset for any town or city to own. It is very scenic and offers serenity for both

51

people and wildlife. The portions from Standley Street to Greenwood Avenue, and from Common Lane to Route 128, are largely protected by Greenbelt and the City of Beverly Conservation Commission. A few private lots exist within this woodland, but none are clearly defined.

Special Features:

In the early spring you can find vernal pools and evidence of amphibian breeding. As the season progresses, starting in May and continuing through the summer, you can find many wildflowers, including wild columbine and various kinds of violets, lady slippers, jack-in-the-pulpits, and later in the season, native orchids such as lady's tresses. Most of these wildflowers prefer areas with no competition from grasses, and they are often found on south-facing gravelly outcrops.

You'll also find many ferns, mosses and club mosses on this property. These groups of plants flourish in cool, acid environs where few other plants exist. The most common ferns at this site are the common polypodia or rock fern, which lives on the humus from decaying logs along the rock cliffs, and royal and cinnamon ferns, which live in low wet areas. To become more familiar with the ferns and club mosses of the area,

Eastern Ribbon Snake

52

see the *Field Guide to Ferns,* by Boughton Cobb, one of the Peterson Field Guide Series.

A hemlock-maple forest provides shelter for a variety of woodland birds. You may see or hear Winter Wren, American Robin, Hermit Thrush, Ovenbird, Black-throated Green Warbler, White-throated Sparrow, Louisiana Waterthrush, Scarlet Tanager, Ruffed Grouse, and Broad-winged Hawk, among others. On the ground, watch for the semi-aquatic eastern ribbon snake. Geologic features include Cape Ann granite, erratic boulders, glacial outwash and faults.

A Walk:

Enter at the cable gate and walk down Greenwood Avenue to the first fork. A fire hydrant will be on the right corner. Turn right onto Wood Lane and within 300 feet take the trail to the right. Follow this trail, going straight at all intersections, to Wood Lane, and turn left. Wood Lane will bring you back to the trail intersection with the fire hydrant. This property map depicts one small section of the larger Beverly Conservation Area and its extensive trail network. Please be aware that a number of smaller, unofficial trails have appeared over time and criss-cross the larger official trails shown on the map. You may wish to keep this in mind as you navigate your walk. As you move along, keep an eye out for the Ruffed Grouse you may flush out of the evergreens and into flight and notice the giant boulders and large rock outcroppings that were left behind by glaciers. This area is also excellent for mountain biking and snowshoeing, with its open dirt roads and trails interlaced with gentle hills and forest.

FIELD NOTES

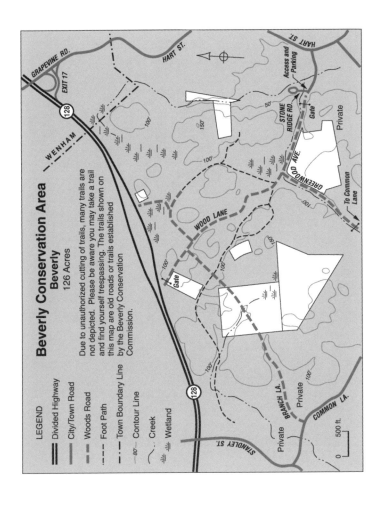

Beverly Conservation Area
Beverly
126 Acres

Due to unauthorized cutting of trails, many trails are not depicted. Please be aware you may take a trail and find yourself trespassing. The trails shown on this map are old roads or trails established by the Beverly Conservation Commission.

LEGEND
Divided Highway
City/Town Road
Woods Road
Foot Path
Town Boundary Line
—80— Contour Line
Creek
Wetland

Dorothy Kerper Monnelly

Julia Bird Reservation — Ipswich

Directions:

From the intersection of Route 1A and Waldingfield Road (a few miles north of Hamilton center and about 1.5 miles south of Ipswich center): Drive down Waldingfield Road until you come to a railway bridge.

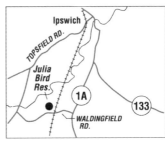

Parking: Just beyond the railway bridge, turn right into a small turnoff. Parking is limited to two cars.

General Description:

The Julia Bird Reservation is 58.7 acres. The property parallels the railroad tracks and extends out to the banks of the Ipswich River. Adjacent to Appleton Farms, it is part of an extensive network of protected open space along the Ipswich River throughout Ipswich, Hamilton, Wenham, and Topsfield.

The Julia Bird Reservation is a good illustration of the effects of different kinds of forest and open field management upon the landscape. The forest in the front area is organically rich bottom-land that supports mature swamp white oak, red oak and red maple, including some trees with a diameter of nearly four feet. This area has not been harvested, and supports breeding birds that prefer a mature forest canopy. A number of standing dead snags also provide habitat

57

for woodpeckers. As you walk further into the property, you will enter an open forest area that has been managed for timber. In 1982, Greenbelt conducted an experimental cordwood cut here, a test to evaluate the feasibility of forest management that does not infringe on other forest uses. Since the cut, we've noticed an increase in the deer population. There is also a contrast in the management of the two fields on this property. The front field has been bulldozed flat and is intensively mowed and fertilized for polo use. The back field shows unaltered topography of naturally flat glacial outwash plain, and is only mowed once a year. Visit this property a few times throughout the seasons and see if you can notice the ways that wildlife has responded to the different types of management.

Freshwater Mussels

Special Features:

In the spring mud season, which typically occurs in March, vernal pools form in the woods, creating the perfect breeding conditions for salamanders. The best time to see breeding activity is during the worst weather: a warm rainy evening in late March or early April. During the rest of the year the salamanders are hard to spot since they live underground. For more information about these subterranean animals, check the website www.vernalpool.org.

Also in the spring, check for Eastern Bluebirds in the hayfield at the back of the property, and Barn Swallows working the front polo field for insects. During the summer breeding season, the mature forest canopy hosts nesting Great Crested Flycatchers, Northern Flickers, American Crows, Blue Jays, Black-and-white Warblers, and Great Horned Owls. In the fall, this property is a staging area for Barn Swallows and green darner dragonflies preparing for migration.

In the winter, the Julia Bird Reservation is great for cross-country skiing, featuring flat terrain in open fields and gentle slopes in the conifer grove at the west end of the polo field. The property also offers good winter wildlife viewing; look for fisher and otter tracks at the river's edge, deer feeding on acorns along polo field edge, and Great Horned Owls in the conifer grove.

Geologic features include Cape Ann granite, glacial outwash, and outwash plain. A layer of clay beneath the sandy and gravelly outwash soils retains the water in the upland areas, providing support for the vernal pools in the woods. Water also filters down through the sandy layer and seeps out as springs at the riverbank above the clay. The gravel-bottomed riffle zone at the bend in the river retains water even in severe droughts, maintaining valuable habitat for freshwater mussels, sponges, limpets and crayfish.

A Walk:
Begin at the trailhead in the parking area, to the right of the Greenbelt sign. As you work your way through the mature woods, you are flanked on the left by a paddock; this area is privately owned and we ask you to respect our neighbor's land. After that, the polo field will be on your left; this is part of the Bird Reservation. When you cross a stone wall and leave the mature forest, you will enter an open woodlot just behind the polo field.

Follow the woods road and note the cut areas on your right; we'll let you judge how well the cordwood harvesting project was conducted. From the woods road, you will enter a hayfield. Turn right and walk around the outer edge of the hayfield, or turn left immediately at the woods' edge. At the front left corner of the hayfield the trail meets the river. Here you'll enter a hemlock stand that shades the banks of the Ipswich River and casts a hushed quiet onto the landscape.

Follow the dirt trail through the woods back to the polo field, or go down to the river's edge and explore the river. Look for signs of beaver activity in the area between the upland dirt trail and the river's edge. When the dirt trail ends at the polo field, follow the right edge of the field to the far end, and enter the conifer grove. Make a loop through the conifer grove, going into the woods and up the hill, and turn left at a black oak. Keep your eyes open for owls, including pellets and whitewash on the ground. Turn left at a black birch and proceed down the hill, noticing a red pine grove on your left. The trail exits the conifer grove on a hillside above the polo field. Go downhill and to the right around polo field edge, with big oaks on your right. Go back into the mature front woods where the trail breaks through the stone wall. Return to the trailhead through the front woods.

Fisher

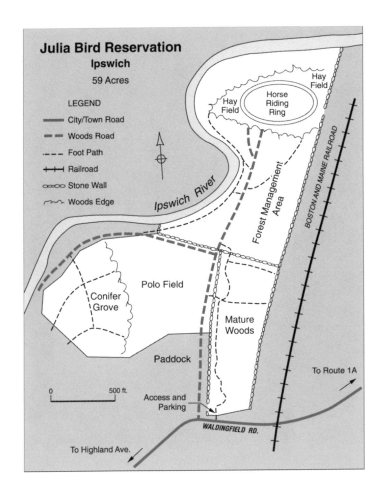

Dorothy Kerper Monnelly

Cox Reservation — Essex

Directions:

From Route 128: Take Exit 15 "School Street" 3.0 miles north. School Street becomes Southern Avenue and leads into Essex Center at the intersection of Southern Avenue and Eastern Avenue. Turn right onto Eastern Avenue, Route 133, and follow the directions below.

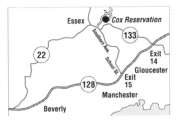

From Essex Center: From the intersection of Southern Avenue and Eastern Avenue, proceed east on Eastern Avenue, Route 133, toward Gloucester 0.5 mile. You will pass the South Essex Center mall on the right, a blinking pedestrian crossing sign, and then make an immediate left turn into our driveway, which is marked by the Greenbelt sign. If you reach Farnham's Clam Restaurant, you have gone too far.

Parking: Follow the driveway over a small bit of marsh, bear right when the driveway forks, and park in the lot above the house by the barn.

General Description:

Located at 82 Eastern Avenue in Essex, the Cox Reservation consists of two parcels: a four-acre woodlot on nearby Lufkin Street, and the 27 acres of upland, salt marsh, farmland with house and barn, and river frontage on Eastern Avenue. The views from the larger parcel east toward the salt marsh, the Essex River, the back of Crane Beach, and Castle Hill and Choate Island are magnificent. The property was given to Greenbelt in 1974 by world renowned muralist Allyn Cox, and serves as Greenbelt's headquarters. The Cox Reservation is the site of several events throughout the year: Greenbelt holds our Annual Meeting in May as the gardens begin to bloom; in June we host Art in the Barn, one of the region's premier art exhibits; and every other year in autumn, we hold Fall Festival.

Special Features:

Situated on the "ancient road" that connected Gloucester and Ipswich as early as the 1630's, the Cox Reservation is an excellent place to study the cultural history of a coastal New England farm. The Burnham family acquired the Cox Reservation land and built the house around 1805, and constructed the barn in 1863. They ran a typical family farm, growing hay and apples and raising dairy cows,

Virgina Creeper and Wild Grape

64

and the woodlot on Lufkin Street provided fuel for the family's needs. The Bacon family purchased the farm in 1907, and planted an extensive apple orchard. Baldwin, Northern Spy, Rhode Island Greening, Ben Davis, and Hyslop apples and a half dozen varieties of pears continue to bear the fruit that provides for cider pressing during our Fall Festival every other year.

Allyn Cox bought the farm in 1940, and converted the barn to his studio in the 1950's, adding windows in the north wall. Cox prepared studies for his major works in his studio barn, and some of these preparatory works have been donated to the Smithsonian Institution. Cox was commissioned during the period of 1951-1982 to paint murals on ceilings and walls for Washington D.C.'s Capitol Building, and his work also adorns Grant's tomb.

In addition to painting, Cox had an interest in gardening, which resulted in a noteworthy collection of perennial flowers around the house and grounds. Old and rare roses, peonies, Solomon's seal, grapevines and an orange tree grace the dooryard garden. Hundreds of other plants have emerged from a tangle of neglect, thanks to the efforts of the late George Anderson and many other volunteers. A large mulberry tree estimated to be over 200 years old shades the front of the house, and on the north side grows a *Rosa mundi* from the garden of Governor William Dudley's ancestral home in Exeter, England.

The farm's proximity to the Essex Bay estuary makes the Cox Reservation a rewarding place for natural history observation. Shorebirds feed on the mudflats off Clamhouse Landing, and herons, egrets, and kingfishers also take advantage of the abundant food source of the salt marsh. The old hayfields host American Woodcock, Bobolinks, and Eastern Meadowlarks; Tree Swallows, and occasionally Eastern Bluebirds, nest in boxes in the orchard and along the hayfield edges. Osprey, Northern Harrier, Eastern Turkey Vulture, Red-tailed

Hawks, and Sharp-shinned Hawks pass through. Other residents and migrants include spring peepers, red-backed salamanders, green darner dragonflies, rabbits, squirrels, chipmunks, meadow voles, coyotes, fox, deer, bats and otters. Dogwood, cherry, honeysuckle, pear and apple blossoms make for a fragrant spring, while hickory, ash, sumac, goldenrod, New England aster and poison ivy blaze against the golden grasses and deep cobalt creeks of the autumn salt marsh. Geologic features on the Cox Reservation include Cape Ann granite, hornblende granite, glacial outwash and erratic boulders.

A Walk:

Starting at the parking area in front of the barn, walk down the road headed away from the buildings. You'll pass through an orchard area with some young apple trees; these antique variety apples were planted in 2000 in an effort to restore the orchard to its former glory. At the end of this first field, peek through the shrubs at the first brushy area on your left; a small quarry, or "motion," is tucked away in the brushy cover. A motion is a common element in the Cape Ann landscape, as

Coyote   Dog

farmers used the nearby resources for their building needs. Foundation stones for the original Cox Reservation barn and stone walls were quarried from this site.

Continuing down the road, you will reach the end of the orchard. A small freshwater marsh along the road here provides habitat for frogs and occasionally Glossy Ibis. Where the road forks, take the driveway to the left. Although the fields on both sides of these roads are privately owned, Greenbelt holds a right of way out to our land on the river. Please respect our neighbors, and stay on the road until you reach the trail on the right which leads to Clamhouse Landing.

Long before the Cox Reservation was farmed, the bedrock ledge of Clamhouse Landing was used to access the Essex River. The landing is also the approximate location where a ferry was operated by William Cogswell in the 1650's. He charged "two pence a person" for this service, connecting the Gloucester side of the ancient road to the Ipswich side. The 165 acres of his farm on the other side of the river, Cogswell's Grant, are protected by the Society for the Preservation of New England Antiquities (SPNEA), ensuring that these historic farm landscapes of Essex will be maintained. A cedar grove shades the edge of the river, and a bench makes this a lovely spot to sit and admire the view.

This is a good place to compare the two most common salt marsh grasses: *Spartina alterniflora* and *Spartina patens*. These two plants provide a visual map of changes in the height of the salt marsh soil. *S. alterniflora* grows where the tide wets its roots twice a day. In contrast, *S. patens* grows on higher ground, receiving only the higher tides each month, and is much finer in texture and grows in flattened whorls like cowlicks. This grass has been harvested for salt hay since pre-colonial times. The heavier *S. alterniflora* was used for roof thatching.

On the way back from Clamhouse Landing, just after you pass the fork in the two driveways, turn left onto the hayfield trail, which will lead you to spectacular views of hayfields and the salt marsh. There are also benches along the way. During Bobolink nesting season, which is May through July, please leash your dog, stay on the trails, and do not enter the hayfields.

You can also launch a kayak or canoe from Clamhouse Landing; the best time for this activity is high tide, in order to avoid a long hike across the mud. Please stop in at the office to let us know you are planning to drive out back, then drive down, drop off your boat and gear, and return to the barn parking area to park your car.

FIELD NOTES

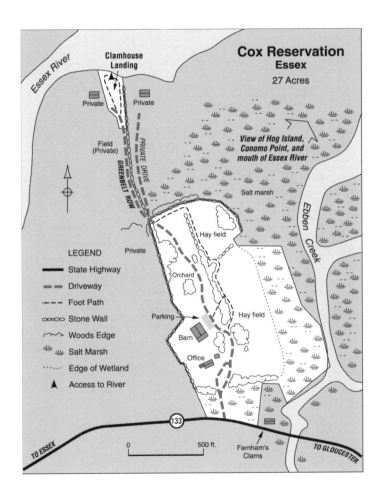

Cox Reservation
Essex
27 Acres

Essex River

Clamhouse Landing

Private

Private

Field (Private)

PRIVATE DRIVE

GREENBELT ROW

View of Hog Island, Conomo Point, and mouth of Essex River

Salt marsh

Ebben Creek

Hay field

Private

LEGEND

━━━ State Highway
╍╍╍ Driveway
--- Foot Path
∞∞∞ Stone Wall
⌒⌒ Woods Edge
⧠⧠ Salt Marsh
····· Edge of Wetland
▲ Access to River

Orchard

Hay field

Parking →

Barn

Office

133

TO ESSEX

0   500 ft.

Farnham's Clams

TO GLOUCESTER

Dorothy Kerper Monnelly

Arthur Ewell Reservation — Rowley

Directions:

From Route 95: Take Exit 54 east toward Rowley on Route 133. Proceed 0.9 mile on Route 133. The driveway to the Ewell Reservation is on the left.

From Rowley: From the intersection of Routes 1 and 133, head west on Route 133 for 1.9 miles. The driveway to the Ewell Reservation is on the right, between the "133" and "slow children" signs.

Parking: Turn in and park along either side of the driveway, taking care not to block the cable gate. Parking is limited to two cars.

General Description:

The Ewell Reservation consists of 31 acres of old field, and young and mature white pine stands. The open field is leased to the Rowley Riding and Driving Club, which maintains the field in return for the use of the property. This upland is situated next to Upper Mill Pond, part of the Mill River system. The waters of Upper Mill Pond are retained by a dam at the northeast end of the pond; wild rice, smartweed, and other wetland plants make this a good staging area for migrating ducks in spring and fall. A sense of peace pervades the quiet woodlands here alongside the pond.

71

Smartweed Family
Polygonum

Special Features:

Ewell Reservation is a prime location to enjoy the splendor and beauty of waterfowl during the spring migration when the ducks are courting. Scan Upper Mill Pond with binoculars. If the light is right, you might see the dazzling iridescent plumage of Ring-neck Ducks, Buffleheads, Hooded Mergansers, Mallards, and Wood Ducks. You may also see Black Ducks, Gadwalls, American Wigeon, Green-winged and Blue-winged Teal, and Pintails. This list does not include all the ducks you can find here, but these are the most frequently encountered at freshwater ponds just after the ice melts in spring.

Plan to arrive before sunrise in the spring for a chance to glimpse otters at the trail edges around the pond. Otters are crepuscular – active during the twilight times before dawn and after dusk. In spring and summer, listen for the dry trill of Pine Warblers in the woods, and look for ant lions at the sandy edges of the field. Look for roosting owls in winter and Pileated Woodpeckers year-round. Old remnants of rushes and button bush exist on the edge of Upper Mill Pond. Geologic features of this property include Boxford Nashoba Formation, Cambrian limestone, glacial outwash, and fault.

A Walk:

As you enter the property, follow the road to a field with a riding ring. Keep to the right of the ring, heading toward the back right corner of the field. The trailhead is between an oak and a white pine. As you enter this mature woods, a view of Upper Mill Pond is on the right. An extensive stand of wild rice provides excellent habitat for ducks during spring and fall migrations. Staying within the woods, quietly approach the pond's edge. Stealth is key here if you want to observe birds. Ducks are extremely wary, especially Black Ducks. Walk along the pond's edge; the trail will continue turning left, leading you through younger pine forest back to the field.

FIELD NOTES

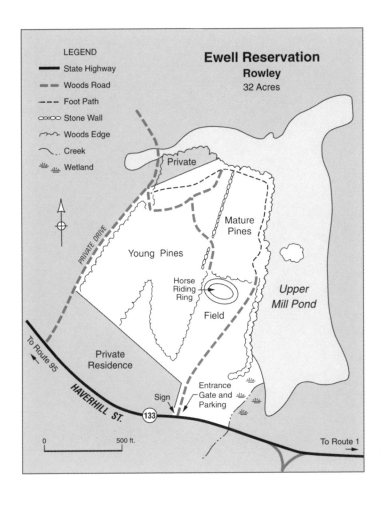

Jim MacDougall

Farnsworth Reservation — North Andover

Directions:

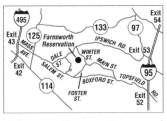

From Route 495: Take Exit 43 onto Massachusetts Avenue and proceed 1.8 miles to North Andover Center. In the center of town, veer left onto Salem Street and travel 0.6 mile to Dale Street. Turn left onto Dale Street and go 1.2 miles to Coventry Lane. You will pass Town Hill Farm on your right along the way. Turn right onto Coventry Lane, and drive 0.5 mile. Turn right onto South Bradford Street, then proceed 0.3 mile to the trailhead on the left.

From Route 95: Take Exit 53B onto Route 97 North towards Georgetown. The very first left will be Pond Street, marked also with a green sign that says Boxford Village. Take this street 0.5 mile, then turn right onto Ipswich Road. Drive 4.8 miles on Ipswich Road, which becomes Dale Street at the Winter Street intersection. Proceed 1.0 mile on Dale Street to Coventry Lane. You will pass Smolak Farm on your right along the way. Turn left onto Coventry Lane, and follow for 0.5 mile. Turn right onto South Bradford Street, then proceed 0.3 mile to the trailhead on the left.

Parking: Park on South Bradford, on the same side as the entrance to the woods. Be aware of traffic speeding around the blind curve of South Bradford. Parking is limited to four cars.

General Description:

Salamander Egg Mass

Farnsworth Reservation is 213 acres. Adjacent to Town Farm, the property forms a greenbelt with the state agricultural preservation restriction on Smolak Farm, state wetlands alongside Bruin Hill, and town conservation land. The Farnsworth Reservation is a good illustration of the effects of residential development on the landscape. Once, a network of woods roads provided access through the contiguous forests here, and sensitive wetlands and vernal pools had a buffer of woodland habitat surrounding them. However, residential development has fragmented this area and introduced several problems: trails are disconnected; exotic plant species escape yards and invade the natural areas; roaming housecats impact ground-nesting bird populations; and runoff from chemical treatment of lawns affects adjacent wetlands and vernal pools. This land has been through many changes since colonial times, going through cycles of clear-cutting, grazing, reforestation and burning.

Special Features:

Look for vernal pools, sedge meadow, Great Horned Owls, and snakes on this property. During drier months, a vernal pool may appear as a depression in a wooded area. See if you can find signs of where the water has been. For more information on vernal pools, consult the Cape Ann Vernal Pond Team at www.capannvernalpond.com as an excellent resource. Geologic features include glacial outwash and moraine.

Yellow Spotted Salamander

A Walk:

Great Horned Owl

Begin at the South Bradford Street entrance, and follow the main trail until you get to a vernal pool on your right. You cannot go any further without coming out into someone's backyard, so turn right before the vernal pool. Take this trail over the ridge between two vernal pools and down into a wet area, where you'll go over a boardwalk between hummocks.

Continue ahead, going up a hill to an old woods road. If you go to the left, you'll see stone walls on the left. Look carefully at the structure of these walls and you'll see that they form a circular shape, with an entrance that faces the trail. The walls are the remains of an old sheep pen, built back in the time when all of this land was used as pasture. Another clue that indicates former pasture use is the white pine forest that has grown up since the land was abandoned. After looking at the sheep pen, turn back and walk down the woods road. This lovely old carriage road is bordered by ferns, highbush blueberry, shoots and small saplings of American chestnut, and red oak. When you reach a "T" intersection, turn right. A stand of mature white pines will be on your right; look for Great Horned Owl pellets below these conifers. To your left, on the other side of a stone wall, is an open field and Mosquito Brook. This is not Greenbelt land; please enjoy the view from the trail, but respect our neighbors' privacy. This old road will take you to a gravel right of way that goes up onto Lancaster Circle. Turn right on Lancaster, then right on South Bradford. Your car will be ahead on the right side of the road.

FIELD NOTES

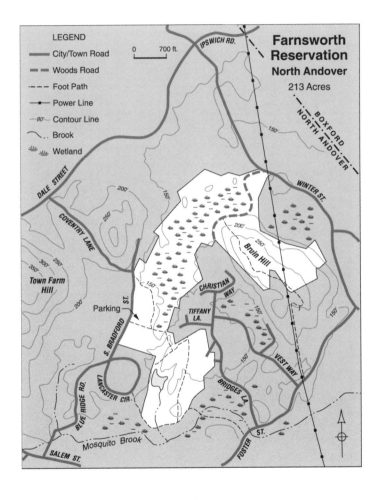

Dorothy Kerper Monnelly

Goose Cove Reservation — Gloucester

Directions:

From 128, at Grant Circle in Gloucester: Drive north on Washington Street, Route 127, toward Lanesville for 1.9 miles. Landmarks you will pass are: the hospital on your left, the Ralph O'Malley Middle School on your right, you will drive over a causeway, and pass The Grange on your right, and a sign for the Beeman School. The Goose Cove parking area is on the right. This is a blind right turn that could be easy to miss. If you pass a small brick municipal building on the right, you have gone too far.

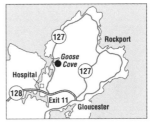

Parking: Park in the dirt lot. Parking is limited to 5 cars.

General Description:

Goose Cove Reservation consists of 26 acres. The property was conserved by the late Dr. Frederic Breed and nearly 500 Gloucester residents who cherished the natural scenic beauty of this woodland as seen from the Goose Cove causeway of Route 127. They united and purchased the land for conservation. As you approach, try to form a mental picture of what this land would look like if these farsighted individuals had not offered an alternative to development.

83

Special Features:

This property features wooded upland, rocky shoreline, and tidal mudflats. The scenery is some of the most beautiful and tranquil of all Greenbelt properties, and provides an opportunity to study varied plant and animal life. Along the shoreline, you can find a variety of estuarine and marine plants and algae existing in unusually close proximity. In the areas closest to shore and with the highest elevation, you will see the Spartina grasses of the salt marsh. Various species of sea wrack live here as well, having adapted to subtle differences in wave action and substrate.

Fisher Track

In the spring, you'll find shadbush in bloom, and cherries beginning to flower. With these come the first waves of insectivorous birds: the warblers, vireos, flycatchers – some of which can be coaxed out of thickets with a little vocal dexterity. Farther inland, you'll find juniper, honeysuckle and goldenrod. These plants prefer the high pH of the soil and cannot tolerate shading from taller trees. The effects of erosion can be seen clearly on the rocks of this shore. Odd hollows, grooves and mounds along the rocky shore demonstrate the ocean's impact on softer sections of rock. You will also find a large number of basalt boulders here – slate gray rocks with some flecking of white, and a fine texture. These are remnants of volcanic activity, formed as lava quickly cooled from its molten state. Later, these boulders were carried here by glacial action. As you pick your way across the uneven shoreline you will see broken shells leaching out of the upland soil and covering the upper portions of the shore. The calcium carbonate, or lime, in these shells sweetens the soil and promotes the growth of certain species. Geologic features include Cape Ann granite, horneblende granite, glacial erratics, glacial outwash, and moraine.

A Walk:

The gravelly openness around the parking area of Goose Cove is the result of a developer bulldozing a temporary road into the property before it was permanently protected. Scraggly black locust trees, gray birch and sweet fern maintain a fragile foothold in the exposed mineral soil. From the northeast corner of the parking area, a trail will lead you to the water's edge. Coral lichen, a flesh-pink colored encrustment that grows on poor soil, covers the ground as you begin this trail. The building to your left is a pumping station, constructed as part of the sewer system of North Gloucester. Continuing down to the shoreline, watch for mammal tracks and scat. Fishers and otters both use this area. Quietly follow the path along the shore, watching closely for Black-crowned Night Herons, Great Blue Herons, Snowy and Great Egrets, Black Ducks, and Ring-Billed and Herring Gulls. After exploring the shore, continue to the point of land, where you can look out over all of Goose Cove, toward the Annisquam River and Wingaersheek Beach. There is tranquillity where the forest meets the sea. If the east wind should intrude on your serenity, you can find shelter behind a rock and let the sun warm your face while you eat a picnic lunch and watch the gulls reel in the currents above. There is a loop trail that circles this point and will lead you back through the upland forest to the main trail and the parking area.

Black Crowned Night Heron

85

FIELD NOTES

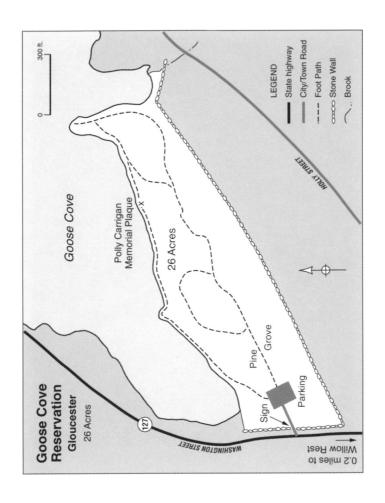

Dorothy Kerper Monnelly

Ipswich River — Middleton, Boxford, and Topsfield

Directions:

From Route 1: Take Route 1 north from Peabody or south from Newburyport to Route 62 West, which is in Danvers. The boat landing is on Route 62, 200 yards beyond a gas station at the intersection of Route 62 and East Street.

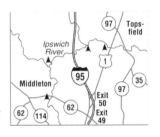

Parking: Park on the north side of Route 62 next to the river.

General Description:

The Ipswich River is a safe, flat-water river that runs from Wilmington to Ipswich. The section of the river described here receives few visitors for most of the year. Get out and enjoy it, but remember that state law requires a life preserver for everyone in a canoe. Currently, most land on either side of the river is privately owned. The county purchased some areas and these have been set aside as conservation land. The Greenbelt lands are shown on the map and you are welcome to land and stretch your legs on them.

Special Features:

Where water exists year-round, one will find a richness not experienced in drier habitats. The riparian ecosystems of the northeast are no exception. For anglers, this stretch of river is stocked with rainbow and brown trout. The best time for fishing is in May through the first

Northern Water Snake

week in June. The river is also a great place to see and hear birds that nest more commonly in riparian habitats than anywhere else, such as Blue-gray Gnatcatchers, Warbling Vireos, Eastern Kingbirds, Swamp Sparrows, Yellow Warblers, Common Yellowthroats, and Baltimore Orioles.

In the past, Native Americans of the Agawam tribe fished along the rivers, as is evidenced by mounds of shell fragments, known as middens, that can be found along the river bank. You may find other archeological sites among plowed fields, cuts in the river bank and excavations by animals. If you want to investigate, the most likely indicator of a site is chipping waste and bits of pottery and shells. Pre-colonial pottery does not have a shiny glaze or colors other than black, red, white, brown, gray, or tan, and objects are not perfectly symmetrical. Although this evidence is far more subtle than pyramids or ruby-studded gold statues, the excitement of finding an artifact adds a new dimension to the outdoor experience.

The greatest value in an archeological find is in the context or specific location of where you found the artifact. Information such as site and surrounding soil type and depth can be critical in identifying and dating the object. Once an artifact is removed from its site, a great deal of information it could potentially provide to researchers is forever lost. If you find something you suspect might be an artifact, please let us know, and we can put you in touch with researchers who can advise you as to the best way to proceed to get the greatest knowledge and value from your find.

Geologic features include Windsor soils which support the flood plain forests of the Ipswich River. These are deep sandy soils with a layer of organic muck. They offer very extensive aquifers that recharge the river with water during times of the year with little to no rain. One way of assessing the influx of water is to wade the river during the summer. You will feel areas of cooler water from springs which dump cold groundwater into the main stem of the river. Eskers and areas of glacial outwash can also be seen along the river.

A Paddle:

Starting from the Route 62 boat landing in Middleton, head downstream. If you have someone to pick you up at another location, you may want to do the 5.4 mile trip to the take-out point at Salem Road in Topsfield — this is a small bridge just upstream from the big bridge on Route 1 at the Topsfield Fairgrounds.

Distances for shorter trips from the Route 62 boat landing are: 2 miles to the Peabody Street/Squash Field access, or 4.2 miles to the Lampert Memorial Canoe landing on Rowley Bridge Road. Greenbelt's Killam Island will be on your left as you go downstream, about 0.7 of a mile after you pass under Route 95. The tall white pines provide a dramatic setting for a picnic, or simply a nice place to stretch your legs.

If you don't have someone to pick you up downriver, you may want to paddle downstream and then return to the launching site. The river is slow here so the trip is relatively easy.

FIELD NOTES

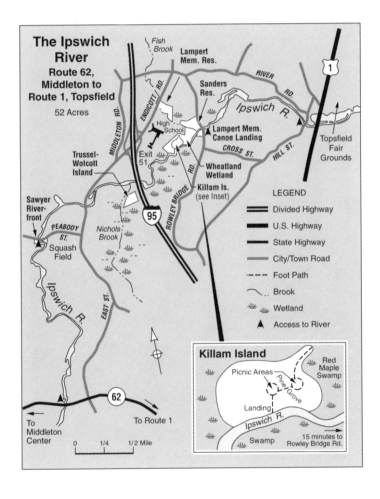

The Ipswich River

Route 62, Middleton to Route 1, Topsfield

52 Acres

LEGEND

━━━ Divided Highway
━━━ U.S. Highway
━━━ State Highway
━━━ City/Town Road
--- Foot Path
⌒ Brook
⚓ Wetland
▲ Access to River

Killam Island

Picnic Areas
Pine Grove
Landing
Red Maple Swamp
Ipswich R.
Swamp
15 minutes to Rowley Bridge Rd.

0   1/4   1/2 Mile

Dorothy Kerper Monnelly

Parker River — Newbury

Directions:

From Route 95 in Byfield: Travel east
on Central Street for 0.7 mile. Turn
left onto Orchard Street and proceed
2 miles until it ends. Turn sharply
right onto Middle Street and travel
0.4 mile to the Parker River.

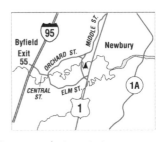

Parking: Park along the road on the
left after you have crossed the bridge.
You will see a sign for Essex County Sportsman's Association.

General Description:

"The Parker River is approximately 23 miles in length and its watershed
covers approximately 82 square miles in Essex County, Massachusetts.
Towns and cities located partially or wholly in the watershed include
Boxford, Georgetown, Groveland, Ipswich, Newbury, Newburyport,
North Andover, Rowley, and West Newbury. Major tributaries include
the Little River, which starts in Newburyport and flows through
Newbury, and the Mill River, which flows through Rowley and joins
the Parker River near Governor Dummer Academy. The freshwater
portion of the Parker River is a favorite angling spot for trout. The
tidal portions of the watershed including Plum Island Sound abound
with fish, and in summer the striped bass and bluefish are much sought
after. The mud flats of the sound are well known locally for their
abundance of clams. There are 14 lakes, ponds, and reservoirs in the
watershed covering approximately 295 acres."

—Parker River Clean Water Association website

Visit the website at www.parker-river.org for an excellent map of the watershed, the weather and tides, fish count data, and other useful information.

Canoeing the Parker River is the best way to appreciate Greenbelt's Cart Creek properties, which include Isabel Hoopes Saltmarsh, Knights Common, and Dyke Meadow. The last property sits next to Great Meadow, 100 acres of conserved land purchased by the Town of Newbury with the assistance of Greenbelt.

Osprey

Special Features:

Apart from serenity, pastoral scenes, and solitude, you are likely to find many birds here – not just any birds, but rare and endangered birds. Waterfowl, snipe, hawks, and sparrows migrate in heavy numbers along or across this river in October. On a good day, you might also see American Kestrels, Merlins, Virginia Rails, Marsh Wrens, Spotted Sandpipers, and various flycatchers, herons, and egrets. Geologic features include Newbury volcanics, Boxford Nashoba Formation, Fish Brook gneiss, and fault.

A Paddle:

The best time for a paddle on the Parker River is in spring or fall, avoiding the peak of the mosquito season in June through September. For a quick canoe trip, launch at Thurlow Bridge on Middle Street about one hour before high tide. Canoe upstream until the tide turns and paddle back out to the starting point, returning no later than 2 hours after the tide has turned. This timing makes for easy paddling and good visibility, and often offers a little wind to ward off any early or late-lingering mosquitoes. For a longer trip, paddle farther up the Parker, past the intersection with Cart Creek, around the next bend, which is Greenbelt owned land on the right, and to a rock outcropping on the right hand shore. This is the beginning of the Great Meadow property. If you would like to stretch your legs, plan to arrive at this point at high water, so you can step out directly onto the rock face. Otherwise, footing can be awkward once the tide goes down. The trails and meadows are off to the left, and one trail is just on the other side of the rock, away from the river. This is a great trip for early Sunday morning when the marsh is waking and begins to sing with life.

FIELD NOTES

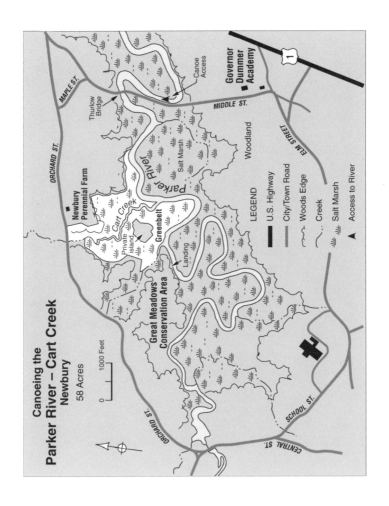

Canoeing the
Parker River – Cart Creek
Newbury

58 Acres

0   1000 Feet

LEGEND

U.S. Highway
City/Town Road
Woods Edge
Creek
Salt Marsh
Access to River

Governor
Dummer
Academy

Canoe
Access

MIDDLE ST.

Thurlow
Bridge

MAPLE ST.

ORCHARD ST.

Newbury
Perennial Farm

Cart Creek

Private
Island

Greenbelt

Parker River

Salt Marsh

Woodland

ELM STREET

Landing

Great Meadows
Conservation Area

ORCHARD ST.

SCHOOL ST.

CENTRAL ST.

99

Dorothy Kerper Monnelly

Rowley Marshes — Rowley

Directions:

From the traffic light in Rowley Center: Drive north on Route 1A for about two miles. Turn right onto a dirt road marked Stackyard Road. When the road forks, keep to the right to stay on Stackyard Road, and drive to the end, about one mile from Route 1A.

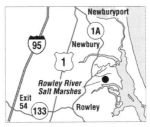

Parking: Park in the Parker River National Wildlife Refuge Nelson Island parking lot at the end of the road. Parking is permitted from sunrise to sunset; no overnight parking is allowed in this lot.

General Description:

Greenbelt parcels in the Rowley Marshes total about 175 acres. The largest single property is the 105-acre Alexander Salt marsh, donated in 1970. The adjacent Bean Salt marsh was acquired in 1978.

The Rowley Marshes are part of The Great Marsh, which extends from Southern New Hampshire to Gloucester, and is the largest salt marsh ecosystem in the Northeast. The salt marsh is the single most important habitat in New England for the production and maintenance of life. As the "nursery" for many marine species including herring, oysters, shrimp, clams, mussels, and many other species of fish and invertebrates, the marsh supports a highly diverse population of migratory and resident birds, and provides two-thirds of the value of our commercial fisheries. The salt marsh also acts as a filter for nutrients and contaminants moving from the land toward the ocean.

For more information on The Great Marsh, a coastal treasure in our backyard, visit www.greatmarsh.org.

The early colonial settlers at one time used the Rowley marshes for salt hay, which was food for their cattle, swine, goats and horses. Traditionally, salt hay was cut and piled on staddles, circular rings of stakes with tops above high water. Today, modern methods of cutting and baling eliminate the need for staddles, and salt hay is often used as garden mulch.

The entire Plum Island Sound ecosystem, including all of Greenbelt's Rowley Marsh properties, is part of a global long-term research project involving 24 sites world-wide. Funded by the National Science Foundation's Long Term Ecological Research (LTER) Network, and coordinated by the Ecosystem Center at the Marine Biological Laboratory in Woods Hole, Massachusetts, Ecosystem Center researchers study salt marsh ecology. Specific areas of study include nutrient and organic matter levels in the marsh tidewaters, water chemistry, and flora and fauna abundance and distribution. The goal of the study is to gain a better understanding of marsh ecology and productivity, and how changes in land use, climate, and sea level, influence these fragile areas.

Greenbelt is an important collaborator on this research project by providing for a long-term lease arrangement for use of our Batchelder's Landing property. Located on the banks of the Rowley River, this property provides the Ecosystem Center researchers with water access, lab space, and housing. Together, Greenbelt and the Ecosystem Center investigators are mapping out strategies for using their data to help communities in the Plum Island Sound area make responsible decisions about land use, in an effort to conserve and protect this incredible natural resource. Visit the website for this research project at www.pielter.org for up-to-date data, analysis of results, and links to related websites. You will find data on water level, temperatures, chemistry, as well as atmospheric data on air temperature, rainfall amounts and much more. The LTER website is a great way to learn more about the Rowley marshes and the Plum Island Sound ecosystem.

Special Features:

The Rowley Marshes are an excellent spot for birding. In summer you will see a host of nesting and post-nesting birds, including Common Terns, Great and Snowy Egrets, Little Blue Herons, Glossy Ibis, Chimney Swifts, Tree and Bank Swallows, Double-crested Cormorants, Sharp-tailed Sparrows, Willets, and Killdeer, among others. Ospreys have recently started nesting on the platform on Nelson Island, visible across the marsh from the parking lot on Refuge land. During spring and fall migrations you might see Greater and Lesser Yellowlegs; Semipalmated and Least Sandpipers; Black-bellied and Semipalmated Plovers; Shortbilled and Long-billed Dowitchers; and many raptors. In the winter months you can see many species of waterfowl, Red-tailed and Rough-legged Hawks, and, if you are fortunate, Short-eared or Snowy Owls. Geologic features in the Rowley Marshes include Newbury volcanics and fault.

A Walk:

In October the salt marsh is awash in color, ranging from the brilliant hot-pink of salicornia to the subtle shadings of golden spartina. Knee-high rubber boots are usually sufficient for walking on the salt marsh, although it's possible that for the more curious adventurers, even chest-high waders will not keep you dry! The marshes are punctuated by mosquito ditches, pannes, and small creeks, so watch your footing.

From the Parker River Refuge/Nelson Island lot where you parked, you can walk out across the dirt causeway to Nelson Island and to Plum Island Sound at the far end of the island, where you have a broad view of Plum Island. Or you can follow the federal boundary signs off to the right, which will lead you out to the marshes of the Rowley River. Just east of this property you should find two old sinkholes used by duck hunters of the past.

Please note that during duck hunting season, Sunday is the only day you are permitted to walk out to Nelson Island, as the Refuge is closed to the general public Monday through Saturday. Be sure to check the hunting abstracts published by Massachusetts Division of Fisheries and Wildlife, or visit their website at www.masswildlife.org to verify migratory bird and waterfowl seasons. The Parker River National Wildlife Refuge can be reached at 978-465-5753.

Great Egret

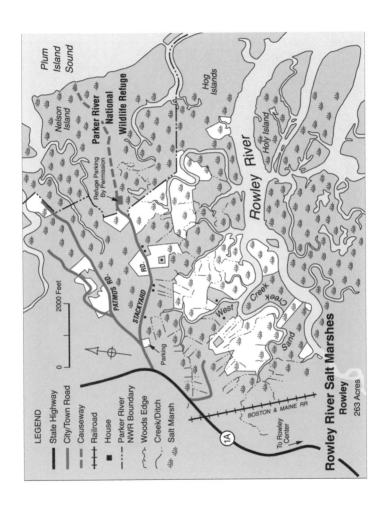

LEGEND

State Highway
City/Town Road
Causeway
Railroad
House
Parker River NWR Boundary
Woods Edge
Creek/Ditch
Salt Marsh

0   2000 Feet

Plum Island Sound

Nelson Island

Parker River National Wildlife Refuge

Refuge Parking By Permission

PATMOS RD.

STACKYARD RD.

Parking

Hog Islands

Holy Island

Rowley River

West Creek

Sand Creek

BOSTON & MAINE RR

To Rowley Center

1A

Rowley River Salt Marshes
Rowley
263 Acres

Dorothy Kerper Monnelly

Sawyer's Island — Rowley

Directions:

From the traffic light in Rowley Center:
Drive north on Route 1A for about two
miles. Turn right onto a dirt road
marked Stackyard Road. When the road
forks, look for the Greenbelt
sign marking the parking pullout
immediately on the right.

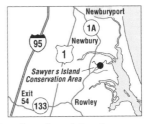

Parking: Park in the turnout on the right of Stackyard Road, across
from the forked intersection where Patmos Road turns to the left.
There is no parking on Sawyer's Island itself, but it's a very pretty
mile-long walk from the pullout on Stackyard Road to the Island.
Alternatively, you can drive out to the end of Patmos Road and drop
off a picnic, a canoe, or your passengers, then return to park at this
turnout.

General Description:

Sawyer's Island sits in the marshes of Plum Island Sound, one of the
most pristine marsh systems in the United States. Much of the land
surrounding the island is protected by Greenbelt or U.S. Fish and
Wildlife Service. The site of the former Salem Boys Camp, the island
is bordered by Sawyer Creek and Mud Creek, which curves around
its northern end. The views in every direction are spectacular, and the
details within the panorama are a delight. Stands of oak and hickory
on the northwest edge of the island provide a lovely sheltered camping
spot (prior permission required) or picnic area. A portion of the island
– though protected by Greenbelt with a conservation restriction – is

107

Great
Horned
Owl

still privately owned, and we ask that you respect the fence-marked boundary.

Special Features:

There are a number of mammals living on or near the island, and depending on when you go, you may see deer, raccoon, fox, or vole. This area is a major resting and feeding spot for all the waterfowl species of the maritime provinces and northern New England during spring and fall migrations. On the island itself you may see phoebes, many types of warblers, vireos, and Great Horned Owls; in the marshes you may find Short-eared or Snowy Owls in winter. In the salt pannes, which are small depressions in the marsh filled with salt water and rimmed with white salt, you're likely to see yellowlegs, other sandpipers, egrets, and herons. These birds often feed near Mud Creek. You may also see many types of ducks and geese.

Along the dirt causeway out to the island, in the marshes, and on the island itself, you'll find a wide variety of plant life. Flowers abound, including several types of asters, daisies, goldenrod, and sea lavender. Salicornia, or glasswort, which grows in the marshes, is particularly noticeable in the fall, when it turns a deep red. It is one of several edible marsh plants. Spartina, the most prevalent of marsh grasses, is what all marsh creatures depend on directly or indirectly. Only about 10% of the standing grass is eaten; the rest decays and feeds a legion of diverse marine species.

In summer months, you may encounter greenhead flies and salt marsh mosquitoes. To be adequately prepared, it is advisable to wear long pants, a long-sleeved shirt, and a hat. As with any visit to deer habitat, remember to check for tiny deer ticks, potential Lyme disease carriers, when you leave. Geologic features of the area include Newbury volcanics and glacial outwash.

A Paddle:

If you're adventurous you can drop a canoe or kayak (see map for launching spot) into Mud Creek, and paddle out into Plum Island Sound. We recommend the months of October or November, when the insects have departed, and when you can float among the scoters, Long-tailed Ducks, goldeneyes, mergansers, and possibly harbor seals.

FIELD NOTES

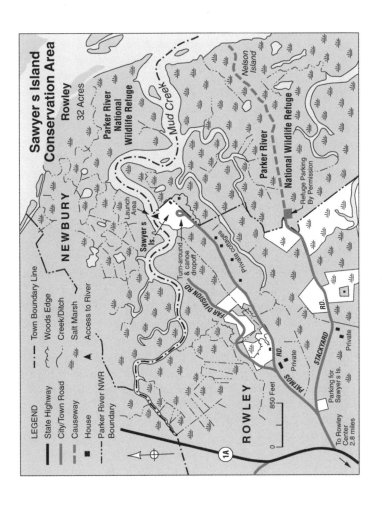

Sawyer's Island
Conservation Area
Rowley
32 Acres

LEGEND
——— State Highway
——— City/Town Road
—·—·— Causeway
■ House
—··—··— Parker River NWR Boundary
—·—·— Town Boundary Line
~~~~ Woods Edge
Creek/Ditch
Salt Marsh
▲ Access to River

NEWBURY

ROWLEY

Parker River National Wildlife Refuge

Mud Creek

Nelson Island

Parker River

National Wildlife Refuge

Refuge Parking By Permission

Launch Area

Sawyer's Is.

Turn-around & canoe dropoff

private cottages

BEAR DIVISION RD.

PATMOS RD.

STACKYARD RD.

Private

Private

Private

Parking for Sawyer's Is.

To Rowley Center 2.8 miles

1A

0   850 Feet

111

Dorothy Kerper Monnelly

Spofford Pond — Boxford

Directions:

From Route 95 and Route 97: Travel west on Route 97 for 0.1 mile and turn left onto the service road. Proceed almost 0.5 mile and turn right onto Ipswich Road. Travel 2 miles and turn right onto Spofford Street, then continue 0.4 mile.

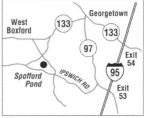

Parking: Park in the pullout on the left by the pond. Please make every effort to park your car so as not to obstruct traffic flow or access to the hydrant in this pullout.

General Description:

Greenbelt protects 27 acres of Spofford Pond and the surrounding area. Boxford has no town water and its fire department depends on pumping water from ponds and streams within the town. The town has created a system of hydrants adjacent to these water resources, and one such hydrant is on Spofford Road adjacent to Spofford Pond. Spofford Pond is a "Great Pond," meaning that it covers more than 10 acres and is under state protection. Greenbelt owns part of the wetland marshes at the north end of the pond, running up to a small esker. Since these wetlands have expanded over the years, exploring the pond is best done by water, not on foot. The waters of Spofford are neutral in pH, which is unusual for this region of acidic soils.

Pickerelweed

Special Features:

Nearly all the primary forms of life can be found in and around a pond: zooplankton, crustaceans, worms, insects, mollusks, sponges, fish, amphibians, birds and small mammals. In the spring and summer, you might see nesting Wood Ducks, or hear an Eastern Kingbird singing like a pied piper. Tree Swallows dart across the pond, snapping up insects, and Goldfinches perform their courtship flight in the

114

uplands. In the past, Least Bitterns have been seen here, but they've been conspicuously absent for some time now. Still, the abundance of Cedar Waxwings, Yellow Warblers, Red-winged Blackbirds and many others make this pond a satisfying place for birding. Mink, muskrats, painted turtles, sunfish, bullfrogs, and green frogs can all provide more treats for the quiet canoeist.

The shoreline is alive with plants. Rosy swamp milkweed, blue pickerelweed, a spattering of purple loosestrife, which is a beautiful but aggressively invasive non-native plant, and white and yellow pond lilies provide lovely splashes of color against the greens and browns of sedges, bulrushes, fragrant sweet gale and water willows. An unusual plant, *Utricularia inflata*, a member of the bladderwort family, is plentiful in these waters. This plant's stem and yellow flower conceal a base of five inflated floating leaves. The leaves contain tiny carnivorous capsules shaped like miniature open clam shells, which snap shut and devour whatever unfortunate creature swims near it, to the horror of resident zooplankton.

Geologic features include Boxford Nashoba Formation, hornblende epidote gneiss, and glacial outwash. Spofford Pond is itself a kettle hole.

A Paddle:

The plants and creatures constitute a dynamic and fascinating ecosystem that makes a trip to Spofford pond rewarding in any season. In the fall, red maples surrounding the pond offer colorful foliage displays, and in the winter, ice provides a roosting place for waterfowl. For an easy paddle that may take 1/2 to 3 hours, depending on your intensity of study, paddle around the pond margins. This is a 28 acre pond and a paddle around the margin would be nearly 0.7 mile.

FIELD NOTES

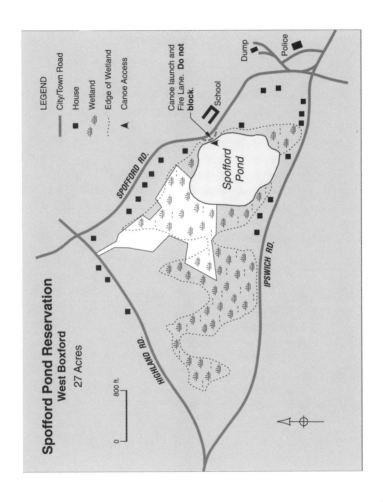

Spofford Pond Reservation
West Boxford
27 Acres

LEGEND

City/Town Road
House
Wetland
Edge of Wetland
Canoe Access

Canoe launch and Fire Lane. **Do not block.**

School

Dump

Police

Spofford Pond

SPOFFORD RD.

IPSWICH RD.

HIGHLAND RD.

0   800 ft.

117

Dorothy Kerper Monnelly

Stoney Cove and Presson Reservation — Gloucester

Directions:

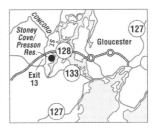

From Route 128: Drive north toward Gloucester. Proceed 0.3 mile beyond the Concord Street, Gloucester exit #13. Watch for the stone pier on the right, before the bridge. Pull off Route 128 into the breakdown lane as soon as you see salt water on the right.

Parking: Park in the pullout off Route 128 just before the stone pier.

General Description:

The 53 acre reservation lies on a bend of the Little River, which joins the Annisquam River as it runs to the sea from the inland side of Gloucester. This property in the heart of salt water farming country combines a colonial history with exceptional ecological value.

Stoney Cove has been a crossroads connecting West Gloucester to Gloucester since the earliest colonial days. West Gloucester colonists had to walk across the marsh, then row across the Annisquam River, to attend compulsory church services at the Green near the site of the present day Chester Grant Circle. In 1694, an initial public route was established by means of a ferry over the river and a causeway built over the marsh to the mainland near the head of Stoney Cove. The current location of Route 128 is superimposed over the old causeway in the immediate Stoney Cove area.

119

In colonial times, wood and lumber were undoubtedly floated and poled down the Little River and the Annisquam River for the thriving trade with Boston, and salt hay left its marshes in heavy flat-bottomed boats called "gundalows." In the late 1800's barges left Stoney Cove at high tide loaded with granite from the quarries off Concord Street. Little Pit was once part of a quarry said to have provided brown granite for St. Margaret's Church in Beverly Farms, was later used as a swimming hole by local children, and is now a tranquil pool of water lilies. Pines grow out of the seams in the granite. Land near Stoney Cove has belonged to a number of Gloucester families, changing hands for "23 pounds, 6 shillings and 8 pence" in 1777, $3600 in 1897 and $110,000 in 1979 when Greenbelt acquired it.

Although the shorter of two wharves is now under Route 128, the remaining pier sees constant use today, with people fishing, bird-watching, picnicking and just looking at the Little River with its lovely view of the marshes and the city of Gloucester in the distance. Clammers work the tidal flats of the Little River today as they have for centuries past, and sailors ply her mid-channel. Stoney Cove is one of the pockets of history which give Gloucester its unique flavor.

Special Features:

The Stoney Cove and Susan's Point area is ideal for the study of successional stages in the life of the forest. Remnants of the old pasture are obvious in the fall and winter. The pioneer trees which settled the old open field, are ground and red junipers, gray birch, and poplars, which must have full sun. These sun-loving species are now being shaded out by hickory, oaks, and maples. The young oaks and maples grow quickly and too close together, showing the "pole" size classification of a timber stand. It is at this stage in growth that a forest manager would do his first thinning of the trees to improve the quality of the sawtimber for a later harvest.

Other successional stages can be seen at the fresh water marsh, which is slowly filling and turning to upland, and in the young pine grove behind the bench. One hundred years are required for a field to turn into a mature forest. What you see at this reservation is a forest about forty percent of the way through the process. The habitats around us are constantly evolving in an orderly progression dictated by soils, climate, fire and man's activities. The complex nature of succession can only be fully appreciated with a good understanding of ecology.

Adjacent to Stoney Cove is the Presson land, which rises from salt marsh to wooded ground and was owned by the same family for 300 years. For a time in the 1800's, the land was farmed and wood was cut there. A family story says that when this was open farmland you could stand on Presson's Point and see all the way to the Boston Light and the Isle of Shoals. The views are still delightful, and the reservation affords fishing, birding, clamming, and picnicking.

Geologic features at this site include Cape Ann granite, glacial outwash, moraine, and fault.

A Walk

Starting at the parking area by the stone pier, follow the trail along the right edge of the salt marsh and up the hill. From the bench at the top of the hill, enjoy a spectacular view of the pier, salt marsh, and Little River below. Look for shorebirds on the mudflats at low tide, and in late September, the bright pink blaze of salicornia in the salt marsh. The Little River supports a herring run in late April to early May; predators such as gulls and otters, which feed on these fish, can also be seen during this time. Following the blue trail blazes, continue past the bench and into the woods, and observe the old stone walls that indicate this land's former use as pasture. The trail will cross one of these stone walls at an intermittent stream; if the stream is dry, you may wish to check the muddy stream bed for tracks. You may be able to identify the heart-shaped hoofprints of white-tailed deer. Shortly beyond the stream, the trail will fork. The loop on the right leads you past a fresh water wetland where Woodcock can be heard on spring evenings, into a mature white pine forest, and then loops around Little Pit. The loop on the left heads out to Presson Point and Susan's Point, past glacial erratic boulders and blueberry patches. Susan's Point often shows signs of river otters along the shore. Follow the yellow blazes back toward the stone pier.

Skunk

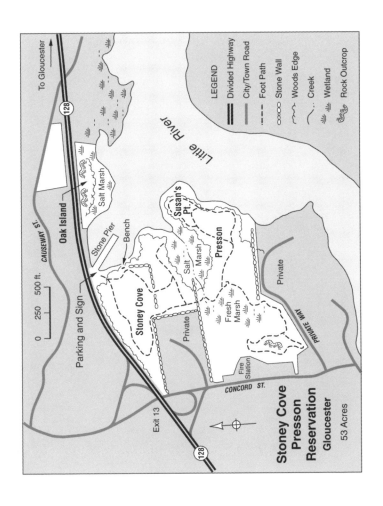

Jim MacDougall

Warren-Weld Woodland — Essex

Directions:

From Route 128: Take Exit 15, School Street, north toward Essex 2.2 miles until you see Bothways Farm on the right, with a cluster of farm buildings at the top of the hill and a small duck pond near the road. Turn left onto Apple Street and follow for 0.6 mile.

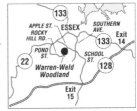

From Route 133 in Essex Center: Drive toward Route 128 on Southern Avenue. After 0.9 mile, you will see Bothways Farm on the left, with a cluster of farm buildings at the top of the hill and a small duck pond near the road. Make a sharp right onto Apple Street and follow for 0.6 mile.

Parking: Park in the small turnout on your left. Parking is limited to four cars.

General Description:

The 106 acre Warren-Weld Woodland is part of the larger Manchester-Essex Woods. The property protects the headwaters of the Essex River, which is a mere trickle at this location, and is part of a wildlife corridor that runs south from the salt marshes of Essex into the Manchester-Essex Woods. For a map of this area, contact The Manchester-Essex Conservation Trust, P.O. Box 1486, Manchester, MA 01944.

There are several natural communities on this property, the predominant of which is an oak forest. Depending on the amount of moisture in the soil, white, red, scarlet and black oaks are interspersed with black birch, red maple, beech, hemlock, white pine, and shagbark and pignut hickories. The slope of the land is generally to the north, creating a slightly cooler climate preferred by beech and hemlock.

Around 1972, this area suffered from an epidemic of hemlock looper. This small caterpillar defoliated and subsequently killed a large number of hemlocks which have since broken at various heights, leaving standing trunks and a tangle of crowns littering the forest floor. When these big trees finally fell, more sunlight and warmth began to reach the understory of the forest. In the late 1970's, the area experienced an infestation of gypsy moths. As these insects consumed oak leaves, and in some areas pine needles, their frac, or insect manure, fertilized the forest floor. The rings on a recently felled hemlock sapling testify to a period of exaggerated growth here in the early 1980's, consistent with the combination of increased light, warmth, and nutrients the understory would have experienced.

The stiff branches of hemlock trees hold the trunks off the ground, so they don't decompose as quickly as other trees. This creates a fire hazard, and the presence of cat briar and low-bush blueberries testifies to some small burns at several points in time. The dead wood also supports a large population of cavity-nesting animals, like flying squirrels and Saw-whet Owls, and wood boring invertebrates. This habitat, and the presence of the wildlife corridor, makes the property ideal for observation of wildlife. Mammals seen here include opossum, red fox, skunk, raccoon, otter, red squirrel, and deer. Remember to check for deer ticks after an outing in these woods.

The co-existence of several natural ecosystems, including a small stream bank, ravines, and an old field community, also contribute to the varied bird population here. Some species you may see are Eastern Towhee, Ruffed Grouse, Black-capped Chickadee, Northern Flicker, Tufted Titmouse, Downy Woodpecker, Saw-whet Owl, American Kestrel, and Broad-winged Hawk.

Ruffed Grouse

Special Features:

A shrub swamp holds several vernal pools which provide a breeding area for amphibians, including spotted salamanders, spring peepers, and wood frogs. If you identify any amphibians here, please contact the office and let us know. Spotted turtles may be seen on this property, particularly in the spring, when they are moving about looking to feed on amphibian eggs. One of the spotted turtle's favorite meals is, interestingly enough, spotted salamander eggs; the adult of this species also has yellow spots. Spotted turtles are basking turtles, and you may see one sunning itself on the tussocks of sedge about the swamp. Several species of wildflowers common to oak forests may be found on the property, such as pink ladyslipper, pipsissewa, pyrola, rattlesnake plantain, bellwort, and wood anemone. You can also see various asters, false lilly-of-the-valley, violets, goldthread, and starflower, along with honeysuckle, bittersweet, and blueberry bushes. The granite outcroppings throughout the woods host stands of the evergreen polypody fern, and areas of lycopodium, or club moss, are scattered everywhere. Geologic features include Cape Ann granite, hornblende granite, and glacial outwash.

A Walk:

Enter the property at the parking area, and head up the wide dirt path, marked as Caesar's Lane on the map. Be careful on the rough and rocky footing along this trail. At the first intersection, keep right, carefully respecting our neighbors' private property on the left. At the second intersection, keep to the center where you'll see bare ledge. This trail will take you to a third intersection; keep to the left and enter a conifer grove. Soon you will reach a T intersection. If is it early spring, the raucous quacking of wood frogs or spring peepers will betray the presence of the shrub swamp directly ahead. If you're feeling adventurous, check out this area. In April, look for frog and salamander egg masses; later in the season they will have metamorphosed into tadpoles and salamander larvae. If you choose not to explore the wetland, please do not use the trail to the left, which leads to private property; instead, go right at the T, and continue on the trail. Head up the hill and turn right onto Conomo Drive, historically a connecting road between Pond Street in Essex and the old road to Manchester. At the next intersection you may go right, and head back to Caesar's Lane and the parking area, or turn left, which will take you deep into the wilds of the Manchester-Essex Woods.

Spotted Turtle

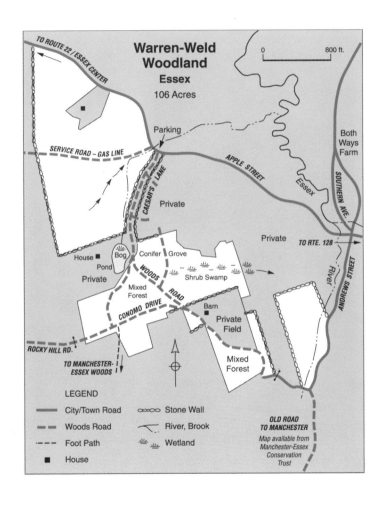

129

Dorothy Kerper Monnelly

Willowdale Mill — Hamilton

Directions:

From Route 1: Drive east toward Ipswich on Ipswich Road, which becomes Topsfield Road in Ipswich, until you reach Foote's Canoe Rental on your right. At the next possible right, turn right onto Winthrop Street. The sign for this road may be missing, but it is directly opposite a large yellow

veterinarian's office. Drive just beyond the wooden bridge over the Ipswich River. The property is on the right and is marked by a small field and pullout.

From Ipswich Center: Drive west on Topsfield Road and turn left onto Winthrop Street. Proceed as above.

Parking: Park in the dirt pullout at the corner of the field, just across the bridge. Do not block the gate, which provides emergency and fire access to Bradley Palmer State Park. Parking is limited to four cars.

General Description:

On 25 acres of woodland off Winthrop Street, along the Ipswich River in Hamilton, the Willowdale Mill Reservation is the site of a 19th century textile mill constructed by Dr. Thomas Manning. The original wooden mill was replaced with a stone structure, and by 1834 a factory complex, including mill, boarding house, and factory building, was in full operation turning out woolen goods. Manning Mills, later known as Willowdale Manufacturing Company, continued making

131

hosiery and blankets until 1884, when the mill was destroyed by fire. Remnants of the mill can be clearly seen – earth, stone and wooden reminders of a century's labor. The sluiceway that channeled water from the Ipswich River to power the mill is dry now, but the once swift current's path is still clearly visible, slicing an indentation from one end of Willowdale Reservation to the other. The surrounding woods are dotted with white pine, with fine broad paths carpeted in layers of pine needles for walking or horseback riding.

Special Features:

The reservation protects 1500 feet along the Ipswich River. Greenbelt owns a fish ladder that allows passage of both anadromous and catadromous fish around Willowdale Dam. Anadromous fish such as alewives and herring migrate from sea to freshwater for breeding, while the catadromous American eels move from the river out to the Sargasso Sea for spawning. Non-migrating fish that inhabit the water include green sunfish, bluegills, pumpkinseed, largemouth bass, yellow perch, chain pickerel, bullhead or brown catfish, and brown, rainbow and brook trout. These non-migrants also depend on the fish ladder, deriving sustenance from the anadromous blue-back herring and returning young eels or elvers. A simple structure like a dam can have far-reaching impact on the ecology of a waterway. Geologic features of this property include Newbury volcanics, esker, glacial outwash, moraine, and fault.

River Otter

132

A Walk:

As you enter the property through the gate, the old mill site will be to your right. Just beyond the cellar hole of the mill is a path leading off to the right over a berm that separates the old sluiceway from the river. The trail is perched atop the earthen dike constructed long ago to channel water from Willowdale Dam to the former woolen mill. On your right is a swift portion of the Ipswich River that is a favorite spot for many anglers. This dike is a well-used path for many mammals foraging along the riverbanks. Observant visitors may spot the tracks and scat of otters, mink, raccoons and skunks.

The trail will eventually lead you to the dam site and the fish ladder. The peninsula on the dam side of the ladder is private, and we ask you to respect our neighbor's property. The trail divides at this point. The trail on the left will take you inland, up away from the river onto a dirt road. Turn left on this road and you will head back to the parking area. The other trail follows the banks of the river upstream. This trail eventually leads you off the Greenbelt property and into Bradley Palmer State Park. The boundary is at the crest of the first rise. This trail is bordered by cedars, hemlocks and pines, creating a very memorable landscape. Cross the small brook in the conifers and turn left. At the dirt road, turn left. Then turn left again onto another, more open, dirt road, which will take you back to the mill and your vehicle.

FIELD NOTES

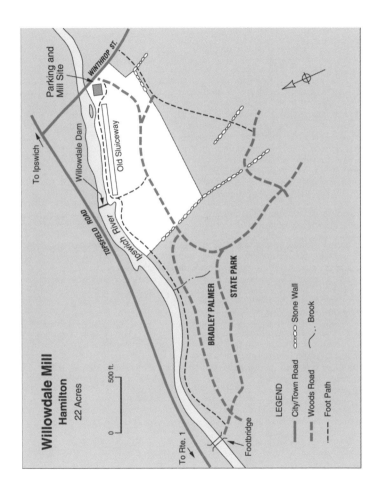

Willowdale Mill
Hamilton
22 Acres

LEGEND
City/Town Road
Woods Road
Foot Path
Stone Wall
Brook

WINTHROP ST.
Parking and Mill Site
To Ipswich
Willowdale Dam
Old Sluiceway
TOPSFIELD ROAD
Ipswich River
BRADLEY PALMER
STATE PARK
To Rte. 1
Footbridge

0   500 ft.

135

GLOSSARY OF GEOLOGICAL TERMS

Geological Features

drumlin: Elongate or oval-shaped hills of clay and gravelly material shaped by glacial movement.

erratic boulders: Large rock fragments that were picked up by moving ice, carried along with the glacier, and dropped when the glacier melted. These boulders are dissimilar to the bedrock type in the region where they are found.

esker: A long, winding ridge of sand, gravel, and boulders. During the ice age, stream tunnels under the ice became filled with gravel and cobbles; when the glacier melted these streambeds were left behind.

fault: Zone of rock fracture along which displacement has taken place. Displacement may be a few inches or many miles.

glacial outwash: Stratified sediment deposited by glacial meltwater, forming sand-plains and gravel terraces.

glacial striations: Straight parallel scratches carved into bedrock by material embedded at the base of a moving glacier.

kettle hole: A depression left by the melting of a block of ice embedded in unconsolidated sediments; it may be filled with boggy vegetation or water.

moraine: Non-sorted, non-stratified sediment or till carried by the glaciers as they moved, and dropped at the end margin of the glacier when it melted.

outwash plain: Glacial outwash forming a naturally flat area.

Types of Bedrock

Newbury Volcanic Complex: Formed about 400 million years ago, this type of bedrock contains fossils from the Silurian and Devonian periods.

Cape Ann granite: Plutonic, igneous rock composed of quartz, feldspar, mica, which was formed about 500 million years ago.

Boxford Nashoba Formation: A type of bedrock which formed about 500 million years ago.

Fish Brook gneiss: Metamorphic rock, typically banded with alternating layers of granular minerals such as quartz and feldspar, and flaky minerals like mica, which formed about 550 million years ago.

Cambrian limestone: Formed about 620 million years ago, this type of bedrock consists of consolidated carbonate muds precipitated from seawater or of carbonate skeletal remains of sea organisms.

Types of Stone

diorite: Intrusive plutonic igneous rock.

epidote: A generally pistachio-green metamorphic mineral.

gabbro: Dark colored igneous rock.

hornblende: A common mineral, forming black to green columnar crystals.

igneous: Formed by lava or magma hardening from a molten state.

intrusive: Igneous rock penetrating older rocks in the form of molten magma.

metamorphic: A rock changed in composition or texture by the action of heat, pressure, and introduction of new chemical substances.

plutonic: Igneous rocks that solidified at great depth; coarse to medium-grained.

REFERENCES

Cobb, Boughton. *Field Guide to Ferns.* The Peterson Field Guide Series. New York, New York: Houghton Mifflin, 1984.

Goldsmith, Richard. *Structural and Metamorphic History of Eastern Massachusetts: The Bedrock Geology of Massachusetts.* U.S. Geological Survey Professional Paper 1366-E-J, 1987.

Cronon, William. *Changes in the Land – Indians, Colonists, and the Ecology of New England.* New York, New York: Hill and Wang, 1983.

Freeman, Stan and Nasuti, Mike. *The Natural History of Eastern Massachusetts.* Florence, Massachusetts: The Hampshire House Publishers, 1998.

Harris, Stuart K. *A Flora of Essex County.* Salem, Massachusetts: Peabody Museum, 1975.

Hurd, D. Hamilton, Compiler. *The History of Essex County, Massachusetts with Biographical Sketches of Many of Its Pioneers and Prominent Men.* Philadelphia, Pennsylvania: J.W. Lewis & Co., 1888.

Kenney, Leo P. *Wicked Big Puddles.* Reading, MA: Vernal Pool Association, 1994.

MacLeish, William H. *The Day Before America – Changing the Nature of a Continent.* Houghton Mifflin, 1994.

Mahlsted, Thomas F. *Pre-Colonial Land Use of Cape Ann.* Presentation at the Essex County Greenbelt Association Annual Meeting, May 20, 2001.

Muir, Diana. *Reflections in Bullough's Pond: Economy and Ecosystem in New England*. Hanover, NH: University Press of New England, 2000.

Murie, Olaus J. *Animal Tracks*. The Peterson Field Guide Series. New York, New York: Houghton Mifflin, 1975.

Raymo, Chet, and Raymo, Maureen E. *Written in Stone: A Geological History of the Northeastern United States*. The Globe Pequot Press, 1989.

Rezendes, Paul. *Tracking and the Art of Seeing: How to Read Animal Tracks and Sign*. New York, New York: HarperCollins Publishers, Inc., 1999.

Sears, John Henry. *The Physical Geography, Geology, Mineralogy, and Paleontology of Essex County, Massachusetts*. Salem, Massachusetts: The Essex Institute, 1905.

Skehan, James W. *Puddingstone, Drumlins, and Ancient Volcanoes: A Geologic Field Guide Along Historic Trails of Boston*. Trustees of Boston College, 1975.

Townsend, Charles Wendell. *The Birds of Essex County, Massachusetts*. Cambridge, Massachusetts: Nuttall Ornithological Club, 1905.

Wessels, Tom. *Reading the Forested Landscape: A Natural History of New England*. Woodstock, VT: The Countryman Press, 1997.

FIELD NOTES

FIELD NOTES

JOIN GREENBELT AS A MEMBER!

Now that you have had an opportunity to read about and visit some of Essex County Greenbelt's beautiful properties, we hope you will want to join as a member, and support our land conservation work year-round!

If you are already a member, we hope you will take this opportunity to introduce a friend, colleague, or family member to Greenbelt's important work of conserving the open space heritage of Essex County.

The benefits of Membership include:

- A copy of *The Greenbelt Guidebook*
- Subscription to the Greenbelt Newsletter
- Greenbelt car decal
- Invitations to walks, festivals, art exhibits and other special events
- The satisfaction of helping to protect our open space heritage for many years to come!

Please use the enclosed resonse form to send in your membership today!